MW01244026

# A Religious Journey
## *The Sun of God*

FRED MARQUIS WORRELL

**FriesenPress**

Suite 300 - 990 Fort St
Victoria, BC, V8V 3K2
Canada

www.friesenpress.com

ISBN
978-1-5255-4090-5 (Hardcover)
978-1-5255-4091-2 (Paperback)
978-1-5255-4092-9 (eBook)

*1. Biography & Autobiography, Personal Memoirs*

Distributed to the trade by The Ingram Book Company

# TABLE OF CONTENTS

# INTRODUCTION

I've been recalling and collecting information about my history and past experiences to set forth this information as an agnostic's autobiographical journey. Like most people, over time I have pondered the meaning and importance of life – What is it all about? This includes some ideas, thoughts, and experiences with religion through my stages of development as a Christian by culture. I was having a conversation with a respected colleague, Professor John Harkness, and told him that I was a Christian by tradition. When I explained it further, he said, "Oh, you're a Christian by culture." I listened to his explanation and have included the term in my writings about my religious experiences. In addition to my religiosity, I've included my teaching and other positions that I've had the opportunity to occupy, and I've taken the liberty to include a selected few of my many anecdotal experiences along the way.

As I was preparing to write, I reviewed some of the material I had read some time ago. As I compiled the information, I wondered if there was any way to make the subject more interesting. Then I recalled my interest, as well as the interest that many Christian theists hold, in the *Screwtape Letters, (Lewis 1962)* in which C.S. Lewis uses a clever technique to make the case for Christianity. I also reread letters from Mark Twain's satirical take on heaven and the Bible in his *Letters from Earth (Twain, 1963)* I like the wit and humor of Samuel Clemens. I've always tried to use appropriate humorous examples when teaching in order to make the information more interesting to my classes when appropriate.

Aha! I hit on the idea of using a similar format to present my autobiographical journey as a Christian by culture. The letter form seemed a little cumbersome, so I chose to write to and receive comments from my friend and pal R. Paul Indrome. The "R" stands for Robert, and those of us who know and like him call him "Bob." So, my comments will be to Bob, or a response to him. Many just know him as Bob. Since Bob and I are both one and the same, I thought it made for a nice guise. Of course, Bob likes to use puns, but maybe I can control his questions and/or comments ...Incidentally, he says that his favorite word is "semordnilap,"and his favorite historical phrase was attributed to Napolean when he said: "Able was I ere I saw Elba".

Along a more serious line, my inclusion of religious information and thoughts has been promoted by my rather recent reading of a *New York Times* best seller, *The God Delusion* by Richard Dawkins (Dawkins, 2006). This isn't an attempt to emulate Dawkins or try to approach his depth of knowledge, research, publications, lectures, and television presentations in Britain and here in the

United States. At the time of writing his book, he was Professor of the Public Understanding of Science at Oxford University, and he's now Professor Emeritus. At last check, I haven't and couldn't accomplish any of his achievements. My approach is to merely select and present information and a few authors that I've found interesting and have influenced my thinking through the stages of being a Christian by culture.

Throughout my career, I've gone through the stages of theism, deism, and agnosticism. The theistic stage occurred during my earlier years with the YMCA in Wilmington, Delaware. While there I met Bill Grace, who was a minister in the inner city. He told me of his frustration to meet the many needs in his church and area without adequate resources. While I considered working in a church, I felt I could serve better by continuing with the Y. He lacked the community support, attention, and resources that I was able to enjoy in my later position with the Canton Community Schools. My deism stage came later as I became more skeptical of the story and tenets of Christianity. I had and have many Jewish friends, and I like the outlook on afterlife by many Jews, but I felt that Judaism was more of a cultural tradition. I visited a Unitarian meeting, which was more in keeping with my Christian tradition/culture with its emphasis on humanitarianism, but ultimately I felt that I could continue as a member of my Presbyterian church, where I had a number of friends. I do wonder if I will be welcomed if/ when word gets out about my agnosticism. We shall see.

The Dawkins book prompted me to write this account from his position on consciousness-raising goals. His presentation reveals his vast knowledge and reasoning. *The God Delusion* is based on his previous seven books and his many public lectures and television appearances in the United Kingdom and the United States. Because he's an evolutionary biologist, some opposed to Darwinism refuse to read Dawkins. Most major Christian denominations and the Roman Catholic Church accept Darwin's theory. They just interject God somewhere along the evolutionary process as the one responsible for the design. Dawkins says he is an extreme agnostic by his scale presented later.

Spencer Wells, author of *The Journey of Man: A Genetic Odyssey (Wells, 2002) became popular* in the early 2000s. It was made into a TV documentary *The Journey of Man (Wells, 2003).* As with Dawkins, I've leaned on Wells for his genetic knowledge, particularly his genetic tracing of Adam and Eve. As I acknowledge Dawkins for his expertise, Well's specialty is also way beyond my knowledge and training. I also want to introduce the reader to a number of subjects and books, including Zoroastrianism, a book about the Bible as history, a book on Sodom and Gomorrah, and a philosophy of religion course that I took at the University of Delaware. I'll introduce a book on the historical Jesus and brief reference to the study group known as the Jesus Seminar.

Additionally, I will mention the influence of Bill Bryson on my writing and teaching. He may help to make my autobiographical journey a little more interesting, as well as reveal many details of science and scientists. I will also include reference to C.S. Lewis, Samuel Clemens as Mark Twain, Einstein, Sagan, Tyson, and lesser household known authors, including Crossan, Keller, Trueblood, and Prothero among others. I have already referred to the importance of Dawkins for my initial motivation. I also like Bryson's book, *A Short History of Nearly Everything*. He spent three years interviewing scientists about everything from the Big Bang to the cosmos and everything in-between. Wow! He presents it all in a way that people can understand, and he uses humorous references. It's is one of my favorite books about science. Bryson draws upon Dawkin's suggestion that the God hypothesis is a scientific one that ought to be viewed with skepticism. I will introduce my Ptolemaic theory of Christianity in the summary and conclusion section.

Because of goals, positions, and writings of many scientists with which I agree, I considered using a nom de plume to avoid being criticized or ostracized by some of my neighbors and friends. I live in a suburban community of about 17,500, in a county of five cities with a total population of about 375,000. Most of the residents won't be typical of those who are agnostics. The Pew Religious Landscape in 2014 reported that about 23% are not religiously affiliated and only about 8% are atheists or agnostics (Pew Religious survey, 1914). I suspect that the actual percentages are higher due to the current stigma as well as time elapsed. I suggest the nonreligiously affiliated are higher among the younger population, as well as differing between regions and other demographic factors. Many of my acquaintances will disagree with my theistic positions, or lack thereof, which was the basis for the original idea of anonymous authorship. I still enjoy attending church on occasion, because it's a venue for me to see old acquaintances I wouldn't typically see. I particularly like to attend the fellowship hour; after all, I've been a charter member of my church since 1960 during my YMCA days.

When I started to write this, I was staying in a very nice house on Marco Island, Florida, on a scenic waterway. When I entered the house in December, there was a Christmas wreath on the door. In the nicely decorated inside was a large cross made of white sea shells on the coffee table. Nearby sat a magazine holder covered by green cloth with "Faith" written in large letters beside a Celtic cross. It was all attractive and I admired the artistry of the sea shells. While I was accustomed to such things and took no offense whatsoever as a cultural Christian, I did wonder what the owners would think about my writing. From all signs, they were among the high percentage who would not agree with me and may be critical. Thank heaven (so to speak) they don't know what I'll be writing when I return.

The purpose of my autobiographic presentation is in no way an attempt to replicate the information or goals presented by Richard Dawkins, Wells, and other eminent scientists and authors. I could not achieve this, as I earlier stated. Readers need to read, think, and arrive at their own outcome. My purposes are:

1. To satisfy myself to set down what I think are some experiences that I found to be helpful to me and my development.

2. To reveal my stages of religiosity, agnosticism, and reasoning over the years.
3. To introduce the Ptolemaic Theory as applied to Jesus.
4. To reveal my history of family, work, experiences, along with a few "woulda, coulda, shoulda" opportunities.
5. To try to make my story an interesting read by way of revealing anecdotal information and experiences.

I encourage everyone to write down their life story, memoirs, or history for themselves, their children, and future readers. My friend Frederick (Rick) Guttroff, from New Jersey, self-published his history and story for his children, grandchildren, and close friends some years before he passed away. I was pleasantly surprised and interested in his story when he shared it with me on Marco Island. I didn't know about his interesting life and experiences. Whether it's a memoir or diary (which my wife, Lois, kept from time to time), or your own story, I think everyone should write it for the record and for their own satisfaction.

I'm known as Fred to my friends and colleagues, but I've chosen to emphasize my middle name of Marquis. It was the first name of my maternal grandfather, Marquis Daniel Cring. He came to live with us via Havana, Cuba, where he was staying with his son Robert and his wife. My uncle, Robert Cring, was a legal interpreter for the United States Fruit Company. Grandfather was an interesting and enterprising person who started a weekly newspaper in Bellefontaine, Ohio, and later became Field Director for Indiana Business College, now Harrison Business College in Marion, Indiana. The Indiana Business College was founded by his brother, my great uncle, Charles Cring.

Grandfather Mark came to live with us after 1941 when Cuba declared war on Germany and Italy. I remember that he was a Mail Pouch chewing, 80-year-old liberal who wrote essays on his Underwood typewriter at a desk near his spittoon. As grandsons, my brothers discussed some of these essays until they were drafted. I was soon the primary beneficiary, since my dad was a staunch Republican and not interested in liberal essays. I perpetuated his name by naming my son and grandson with the middle name, Marquis. My son Rick is a junior; his son Trey is the third. We're all named Frederick Marquis Worrell. Doesn't Frederick Marquis Worrell sound more like an interesting author compared to Fred M. Worrell? Anyway, it's me, or more properly, it is I.

I'm dedicating my story to my wife, and I want to tell you a little more about Lois Jean Gardner Worrell, who died at age 82 when I was 85. She had a genius IQ and when her grade school wanted her to skip a grade or so, her parents thought she was too small and would suffer socially among the larger, older children. Was that a shame, or was it the right thing to do? Her father was a bright graduate of Oberlin College. Not only was Lois bright and an avid reader, she was very attractive, witty, humorous, and full of fun (see pictures).

*— In the Foreword, I state that Lois was attractive and witty.*
*Our wedding picture shows her attractiveness in 1953.*

*— Our Christmas card in 1955. It was her idea to include*
*this picture made into a Holiday greeting.*

Lois was wonderful as a wife and as a mother to our two children. Pam and Rick. We met at church and also attended Kent State University together. She was an art major in the College of Fine and Professional Arts, where she painted in oils and helped me with watercolors when I later decided to take up water-based painting as a hobby. We had a wonderful relationship. We attended lectures together and shared travel, conversations, ideas, and values. Obviously, I miss her dearly! I only wish she were still around to provide advice on what to add here and there, as well as what to delete. The reader would have appreciated her guidance and advice.

# CHAPTER I

## GETTING STARTED

You have brains in your head
Feet in your shoes
You can steer yourself
Any direction you choose
-Dr. Seuss

Do you remember the Cole Porter song "I Get A Kick Out of You" that Frank Sinatra helped popularize? "Old Blue Eyes" tells of suffering from boredom in the lyrics.

That prompted me to make a point about boredom and the word "ennui." I asked six college- educated persons who knew and liked the song if they could tell me the definition of the word without seeing the lyrics. I was surprised to learn that they couldn't, which leads me to think that most of the general public who listened and liked the song had no idea of the meaning of the word. (Maybe the college group were bored with the question.) So, Bob, you and I need to do our best to present information so that the reader won't suffer too much boredom. It will be difficult with all the information I want to present, so here goes!

Bob, before I tell you about me and my life, I want to tell you some things I've learned by reading about religion. To me, the many religions as we in the Western world know them began a long time ago with Zoroastrianism, which many consider to be influential to the formation of Judaism, Christianity, and most world religions that developed out of the Fertile Crescent. I found it very interesting that this religion formed about 3,500 years ago, at a time when there were many gods being worshiped who required different and strange rites. Zoroaster may have been a reformer of the former polytheistic Iranian religion in the 10th century B.C.

The Old Testament mentions some practices that God prohibited. It all began with the god Zarathrusta about 3,500 years ago. The Greeks translated his name to Zoroaster, hence his religion is referred to as Zoroastrianism (Hertz, 1999). It's older than Buddhism and Judaism, and far older than Christianity. Zoroaster was a wise god who preached about personal ethics and was opposed to worshiping all the angry gods of the time with their many sacrifices. He was the first monotheistic god who spoke of good and evil as well as life after death. He said he would return after his death and rule in peace and send his sons after him to rule the world forever in peace. It was a happy and optimistic religion, focused on loving life, supporting one another, serving others, and doing good. With help from Paula Hertz, I summarized most of the above points from her book, *Zorastrianism World Religions:*

1. A personal God that emphasized free will to practice religion.
2. The concept of good and evil.
3. The belief of an afterlife in Heaven or Hell.
4. His return, and later after him, his sons leading the faithful into a perfect world.
5. The first monotheistic religion.

It's no wonder Zoroastrianism was one, if not the one, early religion that influenced Judaism and particularly Christianity at a time when many gods were being worshiped. It still exists where it began in Persia, now with about 200,000 members worldwide. The largest group lives in India (Parsis), followed by the smallest group in the United States. Interestingly, I turned on NPR on the morning of April 3, 2016, and heard the actor Morgan Freeman say, "I am a Zoroastrian." This was the result of his study of world religions with archeologists. He was responding to what he had learned about Zoroastrianism and various other religions.

Bob, you said that Zoroaster sounds like a variety of flower. Well, that may be a good analogy, because it's the root of many religions. The blossoms, however, may be like an allergy or an irritant that lead to more serious consequences, and even death. I could go on and on about the dangers of the blossoms (religious beliefs), as Dawkins does so well, but I'll begin to sound like Chance Gardner in the movie *Being There* (1979) starring Peter Sellers. He played a simple, sheltered gardener who was evicted when his wealthy employer died. He dressed in the owner's clothes and appeared very upper class. He became an unlikely Washington political advisor to the president by speaking about plants and gardening, which along with his bewildered silence was construed as the political analogies of a genius. He became a resident at the home of a wealthy political advisor (Melvin Douglas) through a freak car accident with the wealthy man's wife (Shirley MacLaine). He talked about enriching the soil in order to grow strong roots, and other terms of gardening, which was the only thing he knew. These words were extrapolated and interpreted by those with whom he spoke as having great political significance. He was regarded as an unknown genius.

Pardon me, Bob, for getting carried away with my admiration for Peter Sellers, Shirley MacLaine, and Melvin Douglas in the film, but it's time to make a "reel" change back.

The first book that introduced me to thinking skeptically about religions in general and Christianity in particular, was H.L. Mencken's *Treatise on the Gods.* Mencken reveals the history of religion from pre-history to Christianity, and he generated a great deal of controversy at the time with his genuine scholarship. While best known for his scathing satires, he was an agnostic and felt that religions, including Christianity, couldn't withstand scientific scrutiny. He said, "Reformers were men of courage, but not many of them were intelligent" (Menken, p.242). He was soon welcomed by a new generation of skeptics. Interestingly, the book was recommended to me by my brother Ollie as I entered college. He later became very critical of my agnosticism.

I had to obtain a copy and reacquaint myself with Mencken's book. It's been many years since reading his treatise. I do recall that he stated that all religions were man-made and didn't withstand the scrutiny of science. He emphasized Christianity. I also remember that his style was difficult for me to follow with his many references and extensive use of words. He was certainly a word maven and earned national recognition as a columnist for *The Baltimore Evening Star.* I have learned since from James J. Kilpatrick's *The Writer's Art (Kilpatrick, 1946, p.52)* that one needs to read Mencken "… in small helpings, one spoonful at a time so as not to fall into the clutches of narcotic addiction." This explains my earlier recall of his main points. It took me some time to plow through Menken's treatise. This was the beginning of my skepticism.

Some years later while teaching Sunday school, I found a book entitled *The Bible as History by* Werner Keller, a German journalist who studied the Bible in order to validate its historicity with archeological discoveries. I think it was in the church library, because he makes a statement in the Foreword of the 1955 edition: "The Bible is right!"

Keller's book came out with a revised edition with updates on archeology in collaboration with Dr. Joachim Rehork in 1978. He does a great job going back 4,000 years B.C. to establish the great flood that would have covered that part of the known world. He proceeds forward a couple thousand years to establish credence to the Old Testament, but he has difficulty establishing outside references to verify the New Testament much beyond the Gospel writers. Due to his last admission, I'm sure that his sentiment that the Bible is right was based on his historical research.

Keller's book did a lot for me in that it provided answers to many of my more skeptical concerns of the biblical descriptions. He explains many of the miracles that were performed by revealing facts, conditions, and customs of the time; however, Jesus' feeding of the 5,000 was explained to me differently than the way many people interpret the situation. I heard a guest minister tell the story differently at a time when our church was between pastors. He said that most persons traveling in that part of the world at that time would have food and drink with them. Jesus' miracle was to have all those assembled to share their bread and wine among all those gathered. Obviously, this interpretation of sharing appealed to me as opposed to some kind of "hocus pocus" miracle that many believe.

Okay Bob, I received your command to move on to Moses.

While Abraham is the father of Judaism, it was Moses who returned from Mt. Sinai with the Ten Commandments that God demanded the Israelites obey. It would appear, however, that the commandments were only required behavior among and between the Israelites. Their Old Testament God was anthropomorphic in that He seemed to be a vengeful and wrathful God who led the Israelites to destroy (kill) their non-Jewish enemies. I guess we were to accept this as part of prophecy against false gods. Further, this carried through in their interpretation of a Jewish Messiah who would lead the nation and vanquish enemies. These stories are very interesting, but I need to move on, Bob, and skip your reference to the Mel Brooks movie, *History of the World*, which describes Moses returning from Mt. Sinai with fifteen commandments on three clay tablets, whereupon he drops one that shatters, leaving only ten. Oy vey!

Bob, you asked me if I knew how Moses made his tea. You said, "Hebrews it" (argh). That could literally be the oldest pun.

The Decalogue, of course, is a vital part of the Christian faith, along with other teachings, prayers, and rituals for which the wording may vary between denominations. I know that when I first learned the Lord's Prayer, I said "forgive us our trespasses," but when I became a Presbyterian (referred to as "Presbytyrant" by some who have studied their history), I had to ask the Lord "to forgive our debts." I found it easier to conceptualize "trespasses" rather than "debts." But that's me! Debts and debtors always connoted business procedures to me. Of course, there are many other variations and required creeds, such as The Apostle's Creed, The Nicene Creed (included next), canons, doctrines, confessions, etc. I don't think I'm revealing too much that most readers don't already know, if they are a Christian. I refer to the two main Christian creeds.

## APOSTLES' CREED

I believe in God, the Father almighty,
creator of heaven and earth.

I believe in Jesus Christ, his only Son, our Lord,
who was conceived by the Holy Spirit
and born of the virgin Mary.
He suffered under Pontius Pilate,
was crucified, died, and was buried;
he descended to hell.
The third day he rose again from the dead.
He ascended to heaven
and is seated at the right hand of God the
Father almighty.
From there he will come to judge the living
and the dead.

I believe in the Holy Spirit,
the holy catholic church,
the communion of saints,
the forgiveness of sins,
the resurrection of the body,
and the life everlasting. Amen.

*Apostles' Creed is provided by the Northminster Presbyterian Church.*

## NICENE CREED

We believe in One God,
the Father almighty,
maker of heaven and earth,
of all things visible and invisible.

And in one Lord Jesus Christ,
the only Son of God,
begotten from the Father before all ages,
God from God,
Light from Light,
true God from true God,
begotten, not made;
of the same essence as the Father.
Through him all things were made.
For us and for our salvation
he came down from heaven;
he became incarnate by the Holy Spirit and
the virgin Mary,
and was made human.
He was crucified for us under Pontius Pilate;
he suffered and was buried.
The third day he rose again, according to
the Scripture.
He ascended to heaven
and is seated at the right hand of the Father.
He will come again with glory
to judge the living and the dead.
His kingdom will never end.

*Nicene Creed is provided by Northminster Presbyterian Church.*

Okay Bob, I'll dig back into the archeology of Sodom and Gomorrah.

Keller's book deals with much of the Old Testament, including God's punishment of the cities of Sodom and Gomorrah. He states that the wider area had previously encountered volcanoes and earthquakes, including near the Red Sea. As a result, the water was toxic with salt and oil, and the land wasn't suitable for agriculture. He tells of cliffs of salt that would frequently break off into the water and looked like statues. Anyone walking in the area would soon be covered by a wind-swept dust of salt.

Dr. James Pellegrino, author of *Return to Sodom and Gomorrah* based his research on archeology. He points out that the Old Testament claims that the cities of Sodom and Gomorrah were destroyed by God with devastating fire. It's easy to understand that the cities were in fact destroyed by a Kuwait type of fire with all the oil spewing out in the area.

I enjoyed reading Pellegrino's book. He presents additional information with diagrams of the family trees of primates based on fossil records. They show where Dryopithecus apes spread from Africa to Asia and Europe about 17 million years ago and evolved into other offshoots, including the Australopithecus afarensis ("Lucy"). He describes the evolution of the genus Homo up to sapiens (us) when we arrived on the scene about

50,000 years ago or more recently. Some say it was much earlier than 50,000 years.

I need to mention Homo sapiens neanderthalensis, because there are different hypotheses on what was responsible for their disappearance about 40,000 years ago. Did Homo sapiens kill and eat them? One prevailing idea was that they interbred with modern humans and disappeared, being bred out of existence. Another hypothesis is that the Neanderthals in Europe didn't have advanced tools and weren't as capable of surviving the severe Ice Age. While both may be true, I agree with Wells that they interbred. Pellegrino goes on to describe specific groupings, tribes, and races up to the present day. I may have given this short shrift, for which my anthropology colleagues would take me to task and prefer that I reveal more details of fossil classifications, and dates, but Pellegrino did this extensively in 1994. He would have missed some of the more recent information, including the fossil finds and classification of Homo Naledi discovered in 2015.

While Pellegrino says that his book is the first to ever bring together scientists and theologians to look over Bible stories together by examining the same evidence, he concludes that it's surprising how much they all agree with one another. He adds a chapter on mitochondrial Eve from Africa. She was traced back under the ruins of Karnack, founded 200,000 years ago.

I beg your pardon, Bob, but this has nothing to do with Carnac the Magnificent on the former *Tonight Show* with Johnny Carson. The two names are merely homophones.

Spencer Wells, *The Journey of Man,* traces Eve via mitochondrial genetic markers in females to 150,000 years ago. Yes, Eve existed! Through the same process, Wells traces all males back thousands of years later after Eve existed. He traced the Y chromosome to an Adam about 80,000 years later with a genetic marker that all males have today. Adam and Eve did exist ... they just didn't exist at the same time. This would mean that we are all related to this Adam and Eve.

To move on, Bob, to a more recent time, I want to share one of those interesting conversations I had with Lois when she introduced me to an important book by John Dominic Crossan, who wrote *The Historical Jesus: The Life of a Mediterranean Jewish Peasant.* Crossan was a former Catholic priest who became Professor of Biblical Studies at DePaul University, Chicago, and the winner of the American Academy of Religion Award for *The Cross that Spoke.* Lois and I shared thoughts and skepticisms as she pointed out that the book jacket states: "The Jesus that emerges is a savvy and courageous Jewish Mediterranean peasant, a radical social revolutionary, with a rhapsodic vision of economic, political, and religious egalitarianism and a social program for creating it." (Crossan, 1991, Jacket). Crossan claims that his book was the first comprehensive determination of who Jesus was, what he did, and what he said. Lois thought I would be particularly interested because in his prologue he states that his study was interdisciplinary, including sociology, anthropology, archeology, as well as history. His book fit well with the growing skepticism that Lois and I shared. Major criticism comes from evangelical conservatives regarding his point that Jesus was an illiterate peasant, faith healer, and social revolutionary working among peasants and who would not have called himself "Son of God" or "Son of Man." Of course, during his time and place, his egalitarian preaching ran against Roman-controlled Judea. This would definitely lead to Jesus' crucifixion, which Crossan and others have verified.

Professor Crossan was also an active member of the Jesus Seminar that completed its first five-year report in 1993 on the five Gospels. They reported that their methodological results reveal that 80% of what is reported and attributed to Jesus is inaccurate. A synopsis of their report was presented in *The Canton Repository*, where it's claimed that Jesus spoke of himself as a man, not as a messiah. The paper reports Professor Arthur Dewey from Xavier University, head of the Jesus Seminar, saying that the title of Messiah was given to Jesus after the fact. He referred to sociological analysis, linguistics, history, and archeology to determine the authenticity of more than 1,500 sayings attributable to Jesus by people who believed he was the Christ. They studied Matthew, Mark, Luke, John, and Thomas, including a collection of Jesus' sayings discovered after World War II. There are many criticisms of the reports of the Jesus' Seminar, most but not all from more conservative Christians.

I have to add here that Lois read Crossan's book more carefully than I at the time, which concluded with our old friend, Rev. Dr. Frank Mullen's retirement from Yale Divinity School in 1997. During the reception, Frank, knowing that Lois was an avid reader, asked her, "What's new?" When she told him about Crossan's book, he said to her, "You sure are reading some heavy stuff." That was Lois!

No, Bob, Dr. Mullen was referring to the content, not to the weight of that thick book.

Rev. Dr. Frank A. Mullen was a close friend of Lois and mine, and we often visited with him and Ruth. He was fun and humorous and liked new experiences. He, Lois, and I went to the harness races once at his suggestion. We had fun with $2 bets. Frank was wearing an ascot and fit right in. Later he and Ruth visited us in Ohio on his way from Yale to Richmond, Indiana. Frank was driving a convertible with the top down that summer. He remained the most fun-loving and good friend, known for his good works.

Ruth died of cancer in 1969, only nine years after their marriage in 1960. The *Yale Alumni Magazine*'s obituary revealed his extensive fundraising as development director for the Yale Divinity School. They reported that when Ruth died, he opened his home in Jamaica Estates in Queens to provide safe and affordable housing for nearby St. Johns' college students. Upon retirement, he sold his house and donated the $1.25 million proceeds to Earlham School of Religion to endow its writing program begun by his brother, Dr. Tom Mullen, former dean, college professor known for his good humor, and writing. In fact, Frank sent us *A Very Good Marriage* by Tom because he thought Lois and I had a very good marriage. Frank was

one of our very best friends over the years and admired by
many (see picture).

*Me and Frank Mullen.*

While Frank would disagree with my views, he was a
strong supporter of college students by providing space
in his home in NYC for students who needed a place to
live. He was a very caring and supportive person with his
time and money. Many will remember his kindnesses. An
example of Frank's thoughtfulness was to provide Lois
and me with a special place to stay for his retirement
reception. He arranged for us to stay in Richard Niebuhr's
former cottage, on the YDS quadrangle It was a treat
(see pictures).

*Quadrangle at YDS.*

*Richard Niebuhr's former cottage—left side entrance to YDS Quadrangle.*

Yes, Bob, we had to stay in the closet!

Let's move on to another good book that has greatly influenced my mindset. I met the author and journalist Bill Bryson (via his books) some years ago. He was an American journalist for the British papers *The Guardian* and *The Times* who lived in the United Kingdom. I always found his books to be factual, informative, and full of humor. One of the most informative and most difficult, but nevertheless fun to read, was *A Short History of Nearly Everything*. It's a presentation of science from The Big Bang to the cosmos and everything in between. I love science, from quarks to the multiverse, and I loved his book. It really supports the science of Wells, Sagan, Tyson, Pellegrino, and Dawkins, as well as many other famous scientists to be presented later.

I want to include here a reference made by Dawkins to quantum theory. He quotes Richard Freynman (Dawkins, p. 365), "If you think you understand quantum theory, you don't understand quantum theory." Dawkins further makes a footnote attributed to Niels Bohr: "Anyone who is not shocked by quantum theory has not understood it."

However, Bob, for now I want to get away from the heavy stuff and mention that I have always been interested in many aspects of language as it shapes cultures, and the way individuals think and communicate. While teaching sociology in the early 90s and on to 2013 (yes, I taught classes until my early 80s), I used *The Mother Tongue* by Bill Bryson. It was a great book to assign as a supplement to my introductory sociology class, as it reveals the importance of the English language for our culture and members within our society. Bryson is informative and fun to read, particularly for young people as we discuss youth culture and their language in class. I asked students to raise their hands if they ever got "pissed." All hands went up. Then I asked if they ever tell their parents they are "pissed." Quite a few hands went up. Next, I asked if they ever tell their grandparents they are "pissed." No hands went up. "Why?" I asked. They told me that grandparents think it means to urinate. Point made. As a segue, I was surprised to learn in England that "pissed" means to get drunk. I told the class that some Brits don't say TGIF on Friday. Their term is "POETS DAY" for Piss Off Early Tomorrow's Saturday!

Bryson points out that some cultures have no swear words, and a few others have terms that seem mild to us. The Japanese, Malayans, Polynesians, and Native Americans don't have native swear words. Among the Chinese, "turtle" is the worst possible taunt. Today, the worst words in English are probably "fuck," "shit," and "cunt." The latter was once harmless, and Chaucer used it casually several times in *The Canterbury Tales*. "Pussy" for vagina goes back 1,600 years. "Jock" for penis seems to only survive in "jockstrap."

Bob told me to scratch any reference to "jock itch."

Years ago, I always wondered what it meant when a person said, "I'm all petered out" to express the fact that they were tired. Did it have anything to do with a penis, since it's a term used for that here in the United States? Then I remembered that when miners said that their ore petered out, it meant that it turned to stone; hence, "peter" was used to refer to stone or rock (Greek *Petros*). In Matthew 16:18, Jesus said to Peter "upon this rock I will build my church" (KJV). Was Jesus using a play on words? It was St. Peter's Roman Catholic Church. Penis is called by different names in different cultures. My friend who was at the London School of Economics always referred to her son's penis as "Willy." When we were little boys, our mother referred to our penis as our "trick." I don't know if my mother learned that from her family, but I thought it was a good trick on us boys. Also, I hear a great deal of "shit" these days, so I feel the word is used rather frequently now (including "shit happens" by Forrest Gump's friend "Aging Hippie") as Forrest stepped in some dog poop.

Bob, I swear that I will get back to telling you more about the English language with no more tricks.

If you think the introductory sociology class was filled with only scats and swear words, the chapter on swearing in *The Mother Tongue* was optional of five among the sixteen chapters, including the first two for the student to write up and relate to the textbook for credit. We spent one day talking about all 16 chapters; however, if the reader is interested in factual but humorous uses for the "f-word," I would refer you to the recording by former comedian George Carlin. We'll come back for more Bryson, along with other authors and topics.

Bryson provides information on English words and their uses. He refers to the revised Oxford Dictionary that states the total number of English words to be 615,000, not including scientific and technical words, which may add millions. Educated persons know about 20,000 and use about 2,000 a week. When I presented this information to my class after 2004, I discussed the importance of punctuation by using Lynne Truss' book *Panda Eats, Shoots and Leaves* and this story on the back panel of her book.

A panda walks into a café. He orders a sandwich, eats it, then draws a gun and proceeds to fire it at other patrons. "Why?" asks the surviving waiter amidst the carnage as he makes towards the exit. The panda provides a badly punctuated wildlife manual and tosses it over his shoulder. "Well, I'm a panda. Look it up." The waiter turns to the relevant manual and, sure enough, finds an explanation: "Panda, large black and white bear-like mammal, native to China. Eats, shoots, and leaves." Normally, I don't tell jokes in class, because students remember the joke but forget the point. However, this is a good story to make a point about punctuation.

Bob, I want to share some interesting information from Spencer Wells' about English being one of the Indo-European languages (Wells, 2002, pp 160-170). You said this information was awfully deep. He first makes mention of the popular statement by George Bernard Shaw, where he says that the British and Americans are two people separated by a common language. Wells points out that English is one of 140 Indo-European languages. It belongs to the Germanic branch, with words borrowed from the French. He further states that the 140 languages may be traced to a common homeland people who spoke a Proto-Indo-European (PIE) language. He refers to hypotheses and studies, which include the fields of linguistics, cultural anthropology, and genetics. Wells then traces Eve and Adam back by genetic markers, as stated previously.

These are specialized studies beyond my expertise. He refers to Sir William Jones, who in 1786 was an Indian judge, plus Gordon Childe's work in the 1920s, and Marjia Gimbutas' articles in the 1970s. He includes an article by Colin Renfrew in the 1987 book, *Archaeology and Language (Wells, p.165-6)*. Here he tells us about the homeland of the Kurgan people whose culture was dominated by fierce horsemen who shot arrows while riding fast horses. They settled in the steppes region (now Russia) about 6,000 years ago. They are first mentioned by Herodotus in the 6th century (BC), and originally thought to be the mythological fearless Scythian horsemen.

I found some more interesting things about the Kurgan culture, who were reported to be the original PIE speakers. They buried their dead, along with many artifacts, in mounds known as kurgans. The high status Kurgan people were identified by tattoos. They also used marijuana found in the mounds. They would put hot rocks in a pit and throw in hemp seeds and water, producing a steam of vapors like a sauna for them. I'm sure they were happy!

Bob, I'm glad to end this section on a happy note, as well as the PIE piece.

# CHAPTER II

## YOUNG YEARS

Always remember that you are absolutely unique.
Just like everyone else.
                    -Margaret Mead

Bob, I will pander to you and bear some facts of my young life.

I was born at home in Akron, Ohio, in 1929 (I told you I was old) and grew up in a middle-class neighborhood during the depression. Our house was located near the very edge of the city limits in a suburban area. It was a nice area near a pond known as Brewster Park. A long creek flowed from the pond surrounded by a very large woods where we fished, swam, climbed trees, and skated on the frozen pond during the winter when neighborhood kids would organize to clear the snow from the ice. During the summer when I was between the ages of nine and twelve, I'd leave my house early in the morning with a fishing pole in hand, worms in one pocket, and a peanut butter sandwich in the other. We all knew where to find spring waters along the creek and crab apples nearby, so I could be gone for most of the day with other boys. I had great fun and freedom, almost like Tom Sawyer. I could be gone all day, as long as I was home before father and the family supper. Of course, families almost always ate dinner together. My older brothers had paved my way and could always find me, if I were needed. I think my mother enjoyed the break!

I was the youngest brother of four, ranging in age from one to nine (no girls). We never attended church after moving to the suburbs, but we were a Christian family. My mother had previously been active in a Baptist church, and she read the Bible (religiously) on Sundays. No family member was to work or attend a movie on Sunday. (Of course, we sneaked away.) It was the day of rest. My dad always prepared the Sunday dinner of some kind of a roast and complete meal. In those days, the family would sit together for all dinners (suppers) and usually Sunday breakfast of smoked fish, eggs, milk, toast and jelly, and coffee for parents. I always wondered why our family ate smoked whitefish on Sundays for breakfast. I never asked, and my mother never told me.

I always thought the Cring name, originally spelled as Kring, was German, but I recently learned that we may also be part Scandinavian, a major fish producing area. My brother Bill, a captain, married Lieutenant Camella Bonkrude, a nurse, in Germany in 1945. The Bonkrudes were Norwegian from Wisconsin via Canada and Norway. We didn't know then that Bill and Cam's children, all six of them, were mostly Scandinavian, where the diet includes Omega 3 fatty fish. Bill and Cam and son William Paul died without knowing the possible Scandinavian family influence from the Worrell side.

Yes, Bob, that is my fish tale.

At a very young age, I remember the prayer that many Christian children learn:

> Now I lay me down to sleep
> I pray the Lord my soul to keep
> If I should die before I wake
> I pray the Lord my soul to take

I learned that and the Lord's Prayer later, concentrating on the meaning of the words as they might apply to me, and then to our society and the world. After becoming a skeptic and agnostic, I knew these prayers so well that I would recite them as innocuous words to help me fall asleep. It was a kind of an om-om-om recitation, or as I prefer to think of as ohm-ohm-ohm, instead of counting sheep.

Bob says he's not shocked but is turned off by the switch.

Bob, I have a lot more to say about my dad. He owned a full-size city lot next to our house used for gardening during the summer. It was one of his hobbies and good exercise. It made us popular with the neighbors and provided extra money for us boys selling produce on occasion. I always enjoyed helping to plant seeds, but I did not enjoy the necessary weeding later on. In later years my son learned gardening from helping his granddad. Dad would take me fresh-water fishing in a boat. Additionally, he was a small game hunter and would take us hunting during the fall and winter. I or one of my brothers would accompany him on different occasions with shot guns by age thirteen or fourteen. He always emphasized gun safety. We continued into our later teens, and my three brothers went hunting a few times after they returned from military service. We ate the game, including rabbits, squirrels, and pheasants. I remember picking the shot pellets out of the cooked pieces. I accompanied my dad in western Ohio to hunt for pheasants. I was never successful at grouse hunting in the closer hill regions. I remember their surprising, quick take off, and the loud sound of fluttering wings often scared the hell out of me before I could respond. I haven't hunted since, as I've lost all interest. In fact, I feel sorry for all the animals that we have encroached upon, as some may consider them to be a nuisance. Of course, if a person really needed the food, one could make the case for hunting. Otherwise, the natural sequence of the animal food chain should take care of the numbers, but not always.

I don't want guns in my home today. If I lived on a farm, I'd enjoy target shooting. I taught target shooting for the Wilmington, Delaware YMCA for youths under the auspices of the NRA. The youths and I enjoyed the course, which was fun and emphasized gun safety by using single shot .22 rifles with targets graded for levels of expertise. While Lois and I didn't teach our children target shooting, they learned shooting and gun safety at the Y camp, along with enjoying all the experiences and activities of camp.

Now Bob, before you accuse me of either being loaded or just shooting off my mouth, I want to get back on target to reveal some of my previous aims during my Christian stage.

As a teen, I started attending my parents' Baptist church with a buddy when I was about fourteen. After all, that's where there were more girls than boys. Later, at about age fifteen, I attended the closer Methodist church, because that's where my new girlfriend attended. Before I tell you about membership in the Presbyterian church, I have to tell you about my great YMCA camp experience, which extended into part-time and later full-time YMCA professional work.

# YMCA YEARS

At about the same age that I had a new high school sweetheart, I started attending the Akron YMCA Camp Y-Noah, where my brother Ollie was a counselor during the summers. This was 1943, and World War II was raging. I joined the camp as a junior counselor and proceeded through all the leadership positions over the years up to being (but not) the camp director. We all admired the camp directors, but one assistant camp director stood out for a few years in the 1940s. He was Dale "Zeke" Turner, a Yale Divinity School student who was a dynamic leader, ghost story teller, and athlete at his Akron

27

high school and West Virginia Wesleyan University prior to attending Yale. He gave a few of us senior leaders a framed picture of Christ over a poem by a Japanese poet, Toyohiko Kagawa:

> I read in a book
> That a man called Christ
> Went about doing good.
> It is very disconcerting to me
> That I am so easy satisfied
> With just going about.

Zeke later became pastor of University Congregational Church in Seattle, Washington, where he delivered sermons to his congregation of 1,500 from memory. He took stands on issues such as racism and unwed mothers to diverse members, including Melinda and Bill "Trey" Gates. When Rev. Dale Turner died in 2006, the *Seattle Times*, where he was the religion journalist, and the *Yale Divinity School Journal* printed many tributes to this well-known and outstanding pastor.

After entering college, I worked part-time as a youth director at the Firestone Park YMCA. However, to be a YMCA director (titled secretary), one had to be a church member. I had attended those churches I mentioned, but I never became a member by baptism or taking a confirmation class. So, at age 21, I was baptized at the Firestone Park Presbyterian Church. Some of my former high school acquaintances, a few "Y" leaders, and my boss, the Y Executive Secretary and his family, attended there. It was almost like "old home week."

I'd previously known Earle Gardner, the minister of music, who directed the choir as part of his duties. Earle had organized a barbershop quartet with his friends outside of the church. We'd met a few times earlier when his quartet performed with my group known as The Gay Deceivers (when "gay" meant happy). We were a group of four who entertained by lip-synching Spike Jones records with props and by telling jokes between our records. We started our group at Camp Y-Noah and continued by reputation to earn spending money for college. Two of our group attended Kent State, and the other two went to Akron University. We were all old buddies and got together until the other three passed over the years. My three close friends of our Spike Jones lip-synching group have all died quickly or peacefully. Jack Wilson, age 62, died tragically in a bus crash in New Delhi, India along with four American students while leading a University of Pittsburgh tour in 1996, Dr. Verne Petrie, age 78, from Alzheimer's disease; and Bob Hawkins, a former Akron YMCA Director, died in his sleep at age 82. Isn't that a perfect way to go!? I learned while in Florida this year, the last person from our close YMCA camp group, Jim Heilmeier, passed away on my 90th birthday February 11, 2019.

Our Spike Jones group and Earle's quartet were booked to entertain and raise money for the Akron United Way in 1951. (Yes, at The Red Feather Follies at the Goodyear Theater people paid money to see us!) Earle Gardner's popular barbershop quartet and our group knew each other from previous performances. We appreciated each other's act when we were billed for the fundraiser. Earle was a hip, humorous guy who would often greet us with, "Hi boys! How's it hanging? Are you getting any?" When I started dating his daughter, who sang in the church choir, he greeted me with, "Hi Fred! How's it going? Are you … er … er … ah … ah … doing well at Kent?" I like the story, as Earle had to adjust his old hip greeting to our new relationship.

I was doing fine at Kent State. The Gardner's were a fun, musical family who lived up to (maybe beyond) their income. My family lived at (or below) their income and were older and more occupied with jobs, hobbies, and family. We weren't as highly visible from entertaining community leaders as were the Gardner family. Earle had a higher community profile position as Safety Director with the Akron Chamber of Commerce.

# MY FAMILY ROOTS

My father was William Roy Worrell, born in 1897 on a farm in Hillsville, Virginia, near Galax in Carroll County. I never met my grandmother, Margaret (Maggie), whose maiden name was Liddle, because she died when my father was eight. Later I was able to visit her gravesite at the Baptist church in Galax. The Liddle family history was extensively traced by James Liddle, from Richmond, to William and Elizabeth from Dufton, Westmoreland, now Cumbria. Dufton was a small community located in the Lakes District, where the economy was based on lead mining in the fells of the Pennines. This was about to be an important job for Maggie's family, who migrated to the lead mining area of Virginia prior to the Civil War, or what many Virginians refer to as the Northern War of Aggression. Jim Liddle from Richmond reveals in his extensive, unpublished history that Liddle relatives helped to build the shot tower at Jackson's Ferry on the New River near Wytheville.

Okay Bob, I'll take another shot at discussing more about the Worrell family in the Hillsville area in Virginia. Grandfather George Pendleton Worrell pronounced his name as "Wirl," while other remote relatives pronounced the name as "War-L." I found that the name was spelled Worrall in Cheshire, from where my fifth great-great-grandfather Peter migrated to Chester, Pennsylvania. I was able to trace our name back through his father's direct line to my nineteenth great-great-grandfather John (1295–1360) in Acton, England. The area was known for dairy farming. If we consult Bill Bryson, he points out that if one goes back twenty generations, there are 1,048,576 persons procreating on your behalf (Bryson, 2006, p.397). Of course, this is a HUGE number and assumes that there are no familial intermarriages, with cousins marrying cousins, in-laws, and distant bilateral relatives. For example, we know that Franklin Roosevelt married his third cousin, Eleanor.

I haven't shared my lineage beyond my brother, my own children, and my grandchildren until now. My brothers and I were known by the "Wirl" name in the neighborhood and through grade and high school. The name rhymed with "squirrel" (no comment, Bob). My brothers and I pronounced our name as "War-L" during college, military service, and thereafter. My main college professor was from North Carolina and asked if I was related to the Worrells there. Another professor enjoyed calling on me "as General Sherman said, 'War is hell'". While my surname was pronounced differently by my generation from the previous generation, it did make for some confusion at high school reunions. Some may have presumed our generational pronunciation change analogous to the hoity toity comparison of the spelling of "Fido" as "Phydeaux." It wasn't. It was pronounced both ways by some relatives.

My father received management training by serving on the Goodyear Flying Squadron. The group handled Goodyear dirigibles by moving them in and out of their hangars onto the field with ropes. He literally learned the ropes of management by learning the importance of working as a team to handle blimps in-between management classes. He later served as a division foreman over the Akron plants and was fortunate to have a good management position during the Great Depression. I was proud of my father's success as well as my brothers' successful executive positions or professions.

My oldest brother, Bill, was vice president of a major company and owned two additional smaller companies. He was always considered the brightest because he skipped a grade and graduated from high school by age sixteen. The next oldest, Bob, became a chemical engineer from UCLA and was president of McKay Chemical Company in Los Angeles. My brother Ollie was five years older than I and was living in Naples, Florida before he died at 92 in 2017. He graduated from Ohio Northern University and became a very successful optometrist in the Akron and Cuyahoga Falls areas. The older two brothers died early with cardiovascular disease.

Bill died in Milan, Italy at age 57 while on a business and pleasure trip with Hector McAllister (see picture) and their wives. He was told by his physician not to go because of his congestive heart condition. They were in a restaurant and Bill told them to go ahead and be seated while he sat down to rest. He keeled over and died right there. Because of Mac's influence as President of Firestone, Italy, Bill's wife, Camella, was able to get his body sent back to the States quickly.

Bob died in California at age 68 from a stroke. My dad was 90 and my mother 92 when they passed away. Fred (that's me) had a coronary at 46, open heart surgery at 61, an aortal aneurysm and prostate cancer at age 76, a pacemaker and defibrillator, and a few minor skin cancers since. I broke two ribs in Florida in 2019. I have problems, but I've been able to correct them and get back by watching my diet, exercising, and monitoring my heart. If I'm going to drop dead, I don't know it. Does anyone? My early heart attack was an early warning to make changes.

Perhaps it would be appropriate to be reminded by Goethe's quote, "Nothing is worth more than this day" (Kathryn and Ross Petras, 2016)

Well, Bob, to bore on … my brothers were in World War II. Bill was in the Normandy invasion, where he became a captain and received the French Croix de Guerre and Bronze Star. Bob fought in the Aleutian Islands and was an Air Corps Cadet before he was dropped from training due to the war winding down. Ollie trained as a radio operator and gunner on a flying fortress as part of the Enola Gay project. He stayed stateside. My mother insisted that my brothers had to be baptized at the Baptist church prior to military service. I witnessed it with curiosity, because they were immersed under water. I was about thirteen and glad not to participate. The water looked cold to me.

My mother, Ilo Grace Cring, was born in Delaware, Ohio in 1896. She was the one with the nurturing and supportive roles that provided the glue for our family of six functioning. She often played the piano and taught me WW I songs. Later she taught me to paint in watercolors. She painted in oils and had an art show when she was 80 at Stan Hywet Hall in Akron. While I still dabble, she was a very good artist.

As a family we all attended Cring family reunions held at Mohican State Park or nearby at Dave Elliot's retreat near Mansfield. It was from my mother's cousin a bank president in Mansfield. It was there that I learned a young cousin was called Marky (Marquis). It was hard for one to remember all the names of the many cousins. As the patriarchs died off, so did the Cring reunions.

# MILITARY SERVICE

I had to register for the draft during the Korean conflict. While I was the first of my friends to register, I was the last to enter military service, as I received deferments for a total of five years to pursue my education until age 24. I missed all the action in Korea but served from 1953 to 1955 as a noncommissioned officer. I turned 25 during basic training and felt bad that I was only a private, because all my closest friends were lieutenants. It was a valuable experience to be an older, plain "ol' grunt" among those younger kids. It certainly leveled any feelings of superiority that I may have been inclined to feel as a graduate student.

After training at Fort Knox during a cold winter in a pup tent and marching up "Cardiac Hill" many times, I ended up in the Army Security Agency at Fort Devens, Massachusetts. While in a casual company waiting for assignment, the sergeant asked if anyone had a life-saving certificate. I thought quickly, remembering "never volunteer for anything in the army." I raised my hand and was told to fall out and report to Major Johnson. I told the major that mine was a YMCA life-saving certificate, but we helped train the Red Cross, and I was able to produce a letter to that effect quickly. Major Johnson liked me. (How's my humility?) As a private, I received an appointment as a special services officer as head lifeguard in charge of Robbins Pond at Fort Devens. I was assigned a WAC for the lady's bathroom, and a lieutenant reported to me daily with his work detail to clean up the restrooms and beach area. I recruited four swimmers. I made sure they were better than I by passing my life-saving techniques. What a deal, and I was officially just a private! I could go off base and give swimming lessons at a nearby reservoir for extra money.

Before military service, I was married to Lois and I had soon applied previously for Officer Candidate School (OCS) to keep off Far Eastern Command (FECOM) orders. We were elated when I was assigned as a report's specialist to the 80th Ordinance Battalion Headquartered in Esslingen, Germany. When I arrived in Germany, I was interviewed by the lieutenant and sergeant in charge of reports to the colonel commanding the battalion. (Do you remember that Y directors were titled YMCA secretaries?) They saw that I was a YMCA secretary and asked if I could type. "Yes, sir," I said. Of course, being in school for five years, including graduate school, I typed many papers. I took the typing course while in graduate school but failed the 30 words per minute test without errors. So what? It accomplished what I needed to do my college reports and be a Reports Specialist for the U S Army.

Bob, this was an ideal type of job where I could have a capital experience (as used in Austen's *Pride and Prejudice*).

While at the 80th Ordinance Battalion, I observed discrimination between an American officer and a German employee. At the headquarters section was a large repair shop manned by German-trained mechanics. They repaired motorized vehicles such as jeeps, trucks, and half-tracks. Larger vehicles, such as tanks and self-propelled big guns, were repaired at other specialized centers. The

25 or 30 Germans were housed in a building formerly used by the German army as a communications center. Esslingen wasn't bombed like most cities of 80,000. The mechanics were talented, friendly, and dressed in fatigues identical to ours, minus the small U.S. Army name strip.

The German barracks were inspected by a U.S. colonel representing the Inspector General. I accompanied the colonel, along with one of the Germans as interpreter. He spoke American English perfectly. He looked and talked like an American. We talked back and forth through the inspection with the colonel. At the end of the inspection, the colonel looked at a footlocker and turned towards us and said, "Pretty damn neat for a bunch of goddamn Krauts!" My interpreter friend clicked his heels, saluted the colonel, and said, "If you please, sir, I am a goddamn Kraut!" The colonel was taken by surprise, not remembering that the interpreter was introduced as "mister" and not noticing the lack of a U.S. Army name tag strip. Obviously, he was thrown off balance by the very normal conversations carried on between the three of us. The colonel was probably a WW II veteran, which contributed to his mindset.

Lois joined me in January, and we spent a great year living off base, first in my sergeant's maid quarters and later in a nice apartment in suburban Garten Stadt. We had great opportunities to visit Austria, Switzerland, France, Italy, Netherlands, and historical sights in-between. During this time, we learned some German and met the Martin and Christa Schuller family and became good friends (with the aid of Christa's fluent English).

We continued our close contact and visits with them until they passed away at relatively young ages. During one of our earlier discussions, we told them that we'd be happy to sponsor their two-year-old daughter, Ute, when she became a high school student, if they were interested at the time.

We continued our contact over the years, visiting them several times and following through on our invitation to have Ute live with us for a year. She graduated from North Canton Hoover High School in 1972 as an exchange student and returned to graduate from her gymnasium (H.S.) in Esslingen. While we had learned some German, Ute can speak five languages fluently, including Japanese, for which she has a business orienting and teaching businessmen to interact between the languages and cultures of Japan and Germany. She later married Dr. Hubert Winkels, who is published and well-known as an author and arts critic in Cologne, Germany. Lois and I got to know their children, Andina and Leander, who also speak many languages fluently. Andina received a law degree from the Sorbonne University in Paris. I was very impressed with the vast library of thousands of books in their home in Dusseldorf, which includes many valuable and original paintings. The Winkels family is very impressive. It has continued to be a great experience for my family, which all began with my military assignment to Germany. Ute will visit us again this fall.

# CHAPTER III

## YMCA.

Ubi dubious ibi libertas.
Where there is doubt, there is freedom.
-Latin Proverb

I turned down proceeding to get into the Officers Candidate School (OCS), because an officer had to be commissioned for two additional years of service, and I wanted to return to civilian life. My three buddies were all OCS or ROTC (they called it the Royal Ontario Tank Corps) officers. I applied to be a full-time YMCA secretary and interviewed for jobs in Cleveland and Hamilton, Ohio; in Wilmington, Delaware; in Baltimore, Maryland; in Providence, Rhode Island; and in a nice, smaller city near water in New Jersey. All this took place after I turned down the offer to be executive secretary of the YM and YW in Cuyahoga Falls, Ohio. I didn't think I wanted to be part of a joint YM and YW at that time. I could have had any of the jobs (only one was an executive secretary).

They all liked me (more humility), so I accepted a job as Community Youth Secretary (i.e. director) for the YMCA of Wilmington and New Castle County. I knew Henry Kohl, the executive, and he knew both our families from the Akron YMCA and camp, where I first met him. He and Lois' dad went way back.

It turned out to be a wonderful place to work, where all the professional staff were very warm, friendly, and supportive of one another. We often had dinners together at the Kohl's. Henry's nickname was "Heinie" due to his German heritage. This was an embarrassment to the boy's secretary in the adjacent office, as he said "heinie" meant a person's hind end in this area.

My main supervisor was a PhD from Yale, H. Parker Lansdale III. He was the son of Herbert P. Lansdale, Executive Secretary of the YMCAs of North America. Parker recruited two additional Yale Divinity School graduates. We had one other ordained minister for a total of four ordained ministers out of 13 professional staff. The ministers were more interested in applied Christianity than the politics and required duties of the church. We were all interested in the internalization of religious values as part of our religiosity. This fit right in with my master's degree thesis, which I was finishing at Kent State University while attending post-graduate classes at the University of Delaware. My unpublished thesis was titled *Religiosity and Humanitarianism Among Hi-Y Clubs in Akron, Ohio*. It was an attitudinal study to challenge Clifford Kirkpatrick's study in Minneapolis, where he found that those persons who were the most religious displayed the least amount of humanitarianism *(Religion and Humanitarianism: A Study of Institutional Implications, Psychological Monographs)*. I chose to define a person's religiosity differently by developing an attitudinal survey with a scale to define religiosity as a matter of internalization of religion. He found that those persons who were the most religious displayed the least amount of humanitarianism. I think his findings fit into the idea that people who think narrowly in one area tend to think narrowly in other areas. In my thesis, I challenged his hypothesis by redefining his definitions of religiosity and humanitarianism. My oral defense was accepted.

My job was to organize youth clubs, including Hi-Y clubs, Tri-Hi-Y, Gra-Y, and Indian Guides, in the city and New Castle County. Many clubs included a chaplain as part of their slate of officers. The job went well, with many new clubs in the grade, junior, and high schools. I was also required to assist with the guided tours for youths during the summer with an experienced high school teacher who had led previous tours. We led about 15 youths to Hershey, Pennsylvania, Atlantic City Boardwalk, New York City, and Washington, D.C. Additionally, the Y had a history of sponsoring dancing and social programs (much like some of the Junior League programs) that had been arranged for the fifth and sixth grade boys to learn the social graces with appropriate behavior and attire for dancing and dessert. We still had food fights. After three years, I was saved from this variety of duties, even though I enjoyed it all.

The YMCA of Canton, Ohio asked to interview me to become Executive Secretary of the Town and Country Branch YMCA for Stark County, with an office in the Canton Y. It was a promotion near my hometown of Akron, so I accepted. I was required and had already completed the necessary qualifications for certification as a YMCA secretary, which was required in those years. While doing post-graduate work, I took a religious course, the Philosophy of Religion, at the University of Delaware. Additionally, I acquired church membership and received the required references from my top supervisors, and attended a new special program arranged by the national personnel director in NYC. He arranged for me to take a new sensitivity course through the auspices of the National Training Laboratory in Bethel, Maine, so that I could now arrange training courses for the YMCA. This was a new benefit at that time. Additionally, I took a Group Dynamic course at the University of Delaware. There were just a few of us Y-trainers nationally. (Now can I brag?)

Bob pointed out that I didn't take basic training at Fort Bragg. He said that I had the golden opportunity to train at Fort Knox. Okay, back to basics.

My philosophy instructor at the University of Delaware for a Philosophy of Religion course was an interesting bird. (Aren't many of them?) I was interested in teaching at the time, so I asked what he did before teaching. "I drove a truck," he said. "And before that," I asked. He said, "I ran a gas station." He then told me that he read a lot and had eidetic imagery capability. Of course, he didn't need footnotes if he could remember everything he read. He didn't look much like a college instructor for those days. Did you ever meet any of those guys?

The text that we used was *Philosophy of Religion* by David Elton Trueblood, Professor of Religion, Earlham College. It was a new book at the time. Since it was written by a Quaker, it was an explanation and defense for the existence of Christianity. At the time I had a few disagreements, as he leaned on many of the well-known philosophers, such as Plato, Aristotle, Pascal, and Kant. He also included challenges from Freud, Marx, Lenin, and others. Actually, I felt then and now that he did a very good job defending the existence and relevance of Christianity. In his book, he presents a chapter to reveal that curiosity with reflection is one of the chief features of the natural order among those which substantiate and corroborate the theistic hypothesis. (Trueblood, 1957, pp.79 – 89) Obviously, Dawkins disagrees, with strong evidence to the contrary. Earlier Trueblood quotes Paul Tillich, whose statement regarding God's existence I've always remembered: "God does not exist. He is being itself beyond essence and existence. Therefore, to argue that God exists is to deny Him." (Trueblood, 1957, p.80). The same quote was listed in a *Time Magazine* article with "Is God Dead?" written on the cover.

Bob, you asked me to continue with my "wise" comments.

My experience at the Y in Stark County was similar to my job in New Castle County, except I had more responsibility. In the Introduction section, I told you the size of Stark County (375,000). My job was to organize Y clubs, organizations, and committees in Stark County, outside of the three major cities of Canton, Massillon, and Alliance, but in the 16 villages and the two remaining cities of North Canton and Louisville, in 13 school districts. My board of directors was organized to represent the area and work with the school superintendents, community leaders, and school principals. The latter helped recruit teachers to be advisors for the youth clubs in each school. In some cases, teachers received an extra stipend from the school for "volunteering."

I prepared training manuals and training sessions for all advisors. I found everyone to be very cooperative, so that part of the job was fun. The way had been paved for me, particularly by the Reverend Orrville Briner, who started the Stark County H.S. Athletic Association to arbitrate local grievances and assign all football and basketball officials for the county schools and the two city school districts. My office continued to work with coaches and athletic directors. It usually went well.

Another job that I inherited was running a large day camp and overseeing leaders and buses. There were even burros for the children to ride. One time when the bus broke down, the children were late and parents were concerned (it was before cell phones). It was hot during the afternoon, so as I followed in my car, I drove out quickly to a store and brought back many popsicles. The leaders led songs and the children had a great time waiting until I was able to obtain another bus. The response really helped with the few parental complaints.

My job included an additional assignment to meet and assist with arrangements for the Church Members Luncheon Club, which met at the Central Y. I sit beside David Oyer, one of the former members of that club, when I attend church. All in all, I enjoyed my job and associates, but I was approached by the United Way with a new position with the Canton Welfare Federation of the United Way, directing a new pilot project.

# CHAPTER IV

## COMMUNITY SCHOOL

Its better to light one candle
Than to curse the darkness.
-Chinese Proverb

The Lathrop Community School Pilot Project was presented to the Canton Board of Education by Mrs. W.R.
Timken (Mary) as a cooperative venture to be funded
by the United Fund (now United Way). Her husband
was president and Chairman of the Board, The Timken
Company. The idea was to use the facilities of the
Lathrop Grade School of 800 students for after school
and weekend programs, which were to be programmed
for both children and adults in the district. I feel that I
was selected because of my experience as a community
organizer and the expectation that I would be an applied
sociologist with sensitivity training to work within a primarily black community. It was a busy, interesting, and
demanding job, fighting a turf battle for use of the gym

facility and working long hours, but I enjoyed the people in the neighborhood and the requirements of the job under the auspices of the Canton Welfare Federation, an arm of the United Way. The idea was to program United Way and public agencies to use school facilities after hours and on weekends for the children and adults in the area rather than to build new facilities. It was patterned after a Community School program in Flint, Michigan. An office was created for me in a large space located in the nurse's room at Lathrop School. I had to initially share the school secretary (a fantastic person) until I could arrange for assistance by recruiting volunteers to handle phone calls and registration for classes on site. Until this was accomplished, I was flooded with phone calls while in the office. (Whew!) Other secretarial work was performed at the United Way. I also needed to be out in the community to meet with individuals and local committees in their homes during the day, as well as meeting with agency directors. This included City Recreation, YMCA, YWCA, Adult Education, Ohio State Employment, Welfare Department, Visiting Nurse Association, Family Services, Public Welfare, Public Housing, Health Department and Housing Code Enforcement, and the City Planning Department. Many days the teachers would see me coming in at mid-morning. Some thought I had a great deal! They went home at 3:30ish, and I went home about 5:15 and was back before evening classes. I usually left again about 9:30ish, plus I put in many weekends for youth classes and dances. I always had Sundays off. What a deal! I worked long hours, but I enjoyed it.

For example, one day a little first grader was sitting nearby to see the nurse. She could see me at my desk and said, "You're not working." I said: "How do you know?" She said: "You don't have paper and a pencil in your hand." I mused and told her, "I am a thinker." She thought and rather quickly responded, "You're not working." Bob, I was so busy, the time flew during the pilot project.

Initially, the planning director of the United Way Welfare Federation and I developed a series of hypotheses, with data collection as part of a design to measure the success of the pilot project. We both had advanced sociology degrees and were able to arrange several consultations with the sociology department at Kent State University. This design was very helpful for gathering data and reporting to our board of directors. The board included the Canton Board of Education and five members of the United Way board, their executive director, and the school superintendent. We presented a final report after two years to the governing board and received approval to expand the pilot project at Lathrop to other selected schools, becoming Canton Community Schools with local steering committees. Teachers were hired part-time to serve as directors at each school. This was a major cost-saving change, but it was not as effective as having full-time directors at each school. I moved to the United Way to supervise the expanded program. We were able to hire a very capable director to replace me, Eugene DeChellis, who later became Vice President, Stark Technical College. I replaced Leonard Wilkening as Planning Director and Associate U.F. Director, in addition to the supervision of Canton Community Schools. Leonard moved and eventually became director of Wilder Foundation in St. Paul, Minnesota.

My only real turf battle was with the Canton City Recreation Department. As we used school gymnasiums for local use, they lost the facility for scheduling outside groups for basketball and volleyball leagues. The director continually questioned our attendance data, because he wanted our project to fail. He asked a Board of Education member who was on his Canton City Recreation Board to look in on us. He chose our open house at Lathrop, which was designed to introduce the neighborhood adults to our class instructors in order to sign up for adult classes. As part of the open house, I held youth classes such as dance and sewing, to demonstrate what they had learned in their after- school classes. Well, the gym was crowded with hundreds of people to see the children and sign up for classes. It was reported as a tremendous success at our governing board meeting, as witnessed by one of our board of directors from the Canton City BOE. I had no further questioning of attendance data.

One of my early memorable experiences happened one night while I was working late. It was about 9:45 p.m. and dark outside. I looked out the window and saw five or six black teens hanging around my car. I called home and told Lois that this looked strange to me. I said that I was about to leave, and if I wasn't home by 10:30 p.m., she should call the police and explain the situation. As I walked across the street to my car, one of the youths greeted me and said, "Mr. Worrell, you're working late tonight. We were waiting to make sure you got to your car safely." I never worried about safety again!

Everything continued to go well, with activities operated by private agencies as well as enrollment in youth and adult classes. It was my job to bring in as many private and local agencies as possible through the United Way, school systems and the city, state, and county services. I enjoyed driving through the district and seeing the various agency representatives making their calls. This was a low-income neighborhood with elderly residents. A new program greatly assisting the older population with chores and social services was organized for the Lathrop school district. It was a comprehensive program known as Candlelight.

Yes, Bob, we lit on a matchless project.

# CANDLELIGHT

The City Planning Director, Eugene Bray, initiated the "Candlelight Program" in conjunction with Lathrop Community School. The program was based on the old Chinese proverb, "It is better to light one candle than to curse the darkness." This became a high profile community program involving the Junior League as volunteers and an interfaith youth program. The Candlelight youth program was led by local religious leaders. The youth slept in local churches for one week to help clean and paint homes of the elderly.

The city planning director wanted to develop a housing improvement and rehabilitation program in conjunction with the community school program around Lathrop, with plans to expand to other areas around nearby neighborhoods. He chose areas where housing inspectors found numerous code violations and social problems. The community school was able to help solve the social problems through a social worker and case aides assigned to the program. The entire program was called "Candlelight" and was greatly aided by the Canton Junior League, who, after training, functioned as case aides to assist the social worker assigned by the Family Service Society. It worked well due to the acceptance of the community, the attention received, and the approach to community improvement and tearing down of dilapidated houses. In addition to the social worker aiding the elderly in the neighborhood, a youth program was devised to assist the aged with chores such as cleaning and painting their homes in order to spruce up the neighborhood.

The Candlelight Youth Project consisted of interracial and interfaith youth and adult leaders who served as work leaders and chaperones where the diverse youth worked and slept. Adults and youth slept and ate in an inner- city black church. I got to know and appreciate the African American church leaders and Catholic representatives, consisting of a young priest and two nuns. As a Protestant, I never knew quite how to relate to Catholic nuns. Should I look away? Should I say hello? Should I avoid eye contact? I didn't know. However, after hearing Sister Mary say, "My mother would think I was going to hell in a handbasket if she knew what I was doing here," as she peeled potatoes for dinner, I changed my attitude towards nuns. After the week ended, I looked at all the nuns thereafter to see if I knew them. I came to appreciate all Catholic clergy much more for being down to earth.

I was standing beside the Catholic priest and a Jewish girl painting a house. The priest was very handsome. The Jewish girl asked, "Are you married?" The priest said no. After the priest explained his vows, the girl inquired, "What are nuns for?" You could see what was going on in her mind. They slathered paint with the brush strokes on the side of the house while they talked. It was a learning experience for her and others as they mixed, worked, ate, and slept together in proximity for a week.

In the neighborhood, I met an elderly widow who had $5 left over after she paid her bills each week. I asked her how she got by on $5. She told me she bought a chicken and potatoes and that she ate on it all week. I previously thought I was underpaid. It gave me a real appreciation of what I had in comparison to some residents we were trying to help. I thought I could do more to support the local food bank and push for the government to provide an adequate subsistence for those who needed food, shelter, clothing, and health care in this rich nation.

While I was there for two years, Lois' father died from a stroke at age 53. The Lathrop neighborhood adults took up a collection of nickels, dimes, quarters, and one or two-dollar bills for a total of $15. That gesture greatly touched Lois, her mother, and me, as it was their way of assisting with funeral expenses. The funeral procession to the cemetery was very elaborate because Earle was Safety Director for the Akron Chamber of Commerce and worked closely with the safety forces. The hearse was led by a long parade of police on motorcycles. We heard a person on the street say, "It must be someone important." He was. I remember at the cemetery Dick Harmon, who was an old friend of the family and Assistant Treasurer of Goodyear Tire & Rubber Company, leaned over to Doris and said, "Earle is now up in heaven with the angels," as a word of comfort. While Lois and I realized that this was meant as a consoling comment for her mother, we both had difficulty with the concept of the existence of angels, as well as a place called heaven up there. I will comment on this later as "Binker." Stay tuned!

Within two weeks, I received a call from a former Wilmington Y colleague who gave me instructions to report to the personnel office of the Firestone Tire and Rubber Company, headquartered in Akron. He asked me to come to Akron to meet and be interviewed to be the community relations director for the Firestone plantation in Liberia. I called his boss and told him that I couldn't make a change because of the recent sudden death of my father-in-law, and that my mother-in-law and wife were counting on me to look after the estate and handle all other affairs, as well as provide emotional support.

When I told my brother Ollie, he said, "My God, Fred, Mac is a close friend of mine and Bill's. He's Vice President of Firestone International—remember him? He stayed at the Y. He'd be the very top boss." Was that a "woulda, coulda, shoulda?" I'm glad today that I didn't.

I made the right decision (see picture)! Could this have been a good decision to take Lois, her mother, and our two small children for a great experience? Thinking back, I wonder if such an experience could have been a positive distraction for the grieving Mrs. Gardner.

*On the left is Hector McAllister, who at the time was Director of Firestone International. Later he became President of Firestone, Italy, where he is shown here with Enzo Ferrari and my brother Oliver, on the right. (Picture by Frances Worrell)*

Bob, you said I would soon tire working at a rubber plantation. I think you are stretching a pun.

Meanwhile, back to the community school, where I enjoyed the work with everyone, and Lois and I enjoyed associating with board member Herb Fisher and his wife, Janet. She and Lois had worked together on community projects, like the League of Women Voters. The Fishers provided much-needed extra funds for sewing machines and equipment for youth and adult classes at

Lathrop. He was President of Fisher Foods, a Canton family business started by his father, which spread to five stores and continues today, run by his nephew, Jeffrey. We and the Fishers visited back and forth. On one occasion I heard about Herb's list of relatives to be invited to their oldest daughter's wedding. Janet asked, "Who's Ike Ferguson? He sounds Irish, not Jewish." Herb said, "Oh, that's cousin Ike." He then explained that when he went through Ellis Island in 1930, he was very nervous. When he saw the black uniforms of the immigration officials, he thought they looked like Nazi uniforms. When the agent asked for his name, he froze. The official repeated loudly, "Name?" The cousin responded with "Uh … uh … uh … Ikh fergesn." (I forget in Yiddish. The German " V" is pronounced as "F") Thereafter, Herb's cousin was always known as Ike Ferguson in America. That's the best Jewish immigration story I've ever heard. So many are sad stories.

While I was working at the United Way, I was approached by the Director of the Kent State University Stark Campus, with the approval of James T. Laing, Chairman, Sociology Department. The official title was The Department of Sociology, Anthropology, Social Work, and Corrections. I was approved to teach sociology and social work courses, plus one course in cultural anthropology. All courses required preparation, but I sat in on the latter course taught by an anthropologist, Dr. Bud Shane, on the Kent Campus. After a few years of teaching, I was approached by Stanley Cmich, Mayor of the City of Canton, to direct and work with the mayors, commissioners, and state employment offices that comprised the Cooperative Area Manpower Planning (CAMP) for a six-county district. He was designated by the Department of Labor (DOL) as head of the largest population within the six-county area. His former director had just passed away. This coincided with President Nixon's proposal of legislation to enact the CETA Act (Comprehensive Employment and Training Act), which he later signed into law.

Yes, Bob, I finally got to be a camp director. You sound like an old Y's guy!

I told Mayor Cmich that I would accept on the basis of obtaining a leave of absence from the university. It was quickly approved after the mayor made the request. After I said I would accept the job, and before I officially started, I was approached by a former United Way associate to interview for another job. My friend, who was Executive Director of the St. Joseph, Missouri United Way, wanted to hire me as his assistant to take over his job, because he was in the process of planning to leave. I interviewed with his board of directors but decided not to go as his assistant, because I felt obligated to keep my word to accept the Department of Labor (DOL) position as CAMP director within the mayor's assigned district. My friend left St. Joseph before I began to organize all the various entities. His United Way board president immediately called to offer me the position of Executive Director. It would have been a higher community profile job with higher pay, but I would have to give up my two-year leave of absence from Kent State University, which I had already negotiated, as well as abrogate my agreement with Mayor Cmich. Was this another "woulda, coulda, shoulda?" I'm glad I didn't!

I began the job with an office staff of four and a budget of $4,000,000 to fund the various employment and training programs within the district. Additional grants were made to employ youths during the summer. The youth program was expanded under the CETA bill signed by President Nixon. My office was responsible for insuring that the various funded agencies were operating in accordance with the rules, regulations, and budgets as set forth by legislation. At that point I hired a budget director to keep records of transfers of all funds allocated to the many providers. After all, it's a serious offense to misappropriate federal funds! I found it very interesting to learn how some providers were able to defeat the intent of the law by devious methods. One of the techniques was to go back over the records of recent hires to see if they met the CETA guidelines, rather than to employ new persons as intended by the legislation. This provided the agency with additional dollars, and it wasn't illegal, since they technically met the guidelines.

On another occasion, our office had to call in DOL to investigate a summer youth program for not following the regulations as required. They made the necessary changes to continue their program. While this provided a further learning opportunity for me, I want the reader to know that most of the programs were well run and provided valuable employment opportunities and services.

During this time period, I was approached by my DOL representative in Chicago, who offered me a scholarship award to attend a summer course at the John F. Kennedy School of Government at Harvard. The mayor thought it would be a good career opportunity with the DOL, but he thought I should remain in the fall and not return to Kent State, as previously arranged. I talked it over with Lois and she said it was up to me. My son was entering high school, and my daughter would be graduating soon and entering college, with tuition waived at Kent State University. I thought Lois needed me to help with the children at this juncture, and I really enjoyed teaching rather than more administrative responsibilities within a governmental political framework. The mayor's assistant called me aside and pointed out that under this new CETA funding, I'd be responsible for a $20,000,000 budget, up from the current $4,000,000. "That's a lot of power," he said. I talked to my Dean at Kent State and agreed to return as a Kent State professor of sociology and social work on the Stark Campus. Was that another "woulda, coulda, shoulda?" Again, I'm glad I didn't. It would have looked good on my vitae to be selected for Harvard.

Yes, Bob, I passed the buck again.

I enjoyed getting back to the classroom and interacting with students. I was able to associate the name and face of all 200+ students without making seat assignments by the end of each quarter. It was easier when we converted to semesters. I still remember many students who went on to great success. They had the help of an excellent cadre of colleagues and, of course, their own abilities.

When I told the mayor that I was going back to the university, he understood my decision but asked me not to tell my staff. When I returned to my office, I thought I could tell them by emphasizing the importance of confidentiality until the mayor announced it. All five agreed. The mayor called me the next day and said, "I thought I told you not to tell your staff. Joe was up her early this morning asking to be appointed in your place as director. That's what I was trying to avoid." Well, I learned the hard way how to behave in the political world. One must play their cards close to their vest! Joe didn't get the job, and an outsider was brought in to replace me.

# CHAPTER V

## RETURN TO TEACHING

Avery nice sort of place, Oxford,
for people who like that sort of place.
They teach you to be a gentleman there.
In the Polytechnic, they teach you to be an
engineer or such like.
                    -George Bernard Shaw

Back to Kent Stark, I had additional responsibilities and opportunities as a faculty member required to serve on many promotion and tenure committees and carrying the mace to lead faculty at graduating ceremonies as the faculty processed in regalia. I did this four years for the period while serving as Chair of the Faculty Council. These were jobs required by other faculty Chair members, in addition for all faculty to keeping office hours for students. One additional duty I had was being asked to head the Midwest Writers Conference in 1980. That year I was approached by the Canton Writers Guild, not because I was a known writer, but because many of the members knew me and wanted to expand and use our larger campus facilities, food service, and parking facilities. I had volunteer help from faculty and the guild, plus administrative and secretarial assistance provided by an art's grant we received. While this was additional work, I had the opportunity to meet and introduce the main speakers, editors, and literary agents, from fiction and non-fiction categories. I don't have records, but I remember Robert Newton Peck, Pierre Salinger, Ralph Nader, Tom Wolfe, and George Plimpton being there. All speakers were pleasant, friendly, and available to meet with conferees for the next day sessions.

When I introduced George Plimpton, he was sprawled in a seat a few rows away, looking disinterested and bored as I read off his many accomplishments. I began to wonder if we'd made a mistake by having him as the keynote speaker. He just didn't appear to be the kind of dynamic kick-off speaker we needed to set the tone for the three-day conference. When I announced his name, he jumped up and strode quickly to the dais. After thanking me, he grabbed the microphone confidently and delivered a dynamic and interesting presentation. He was one of our best speakers ever. That's how I remember George Plimpton!

# FULBRIGHT AWARD

I agreed to be the director of the Writers Conference for two years, but was unable to continue the third year because I was accepted as a Fulbright Exchange professor to teach sociology and social work at Trent Polytechnic, now Trent University in Nottingham, England, for the 1982–83 academic year. This took some doing on my part. My partner was John Hort, a Cambridge University graduate in literature. The head of my department, the Department of Sociology, Anthropology, Social Work and Corrections, was a PhD anthropology major from Harvard. He said he couldn't approve John Hort to replace me because he didn't have the minimum of an earned master's degree in the areas that our disciplines required. My Dean passed the message on to me. Doggone it!

I knew one of my colleagues in the English department at my campus was leaving. I also knew her department head on the Kent Campus accepted his type of Oxbridge master's degree, which was based on the Old English Guild system. An Oxford or Cambridge graduate who worked their degree for ten years was considered to be a master and granted a master's degree by application and a small processing fee. So, John was one of those with a master's degree and approved by Britain to replace me. I was a better fit for them by training than he was for me. I was replacing a lecturer, as all 25 were titled in the social science division there at the Poly. He couldn't take over my sociology classes, only a couple of social work classes that he'd been teaching. They used our textbooks there, and the sociology classes were basic sociology with different data for the United Kingdom.

My job was easy, and the pace was slow for me. It was an honors program, with each year level limited to 40 admissions. I also taught a graduate program for nurses and social workers to be qualified for the Certificate to Qualify in Social Work (CQSW) degree. The students at the Poly were graded on two essays per trimester, plus a comprehensive year-end examination. The essays were graded on content and proper grammar and construction. The pass mark was 40, with an average of "C," some "Bs," and very few "As." Very few failed due to competition, prescreening, and the passing of "A Level" exams at the 6th form level (our junior/senior high school high ability level). As government funds were reduced, the funded slots became more competitive. The system is changing at the high school level today to Comprehensive Secondary Education (CSE) certificates for four years, but when I was there, the average school leaving age was primarily still 16.

Since then, our further education systems are structured to be more similar, but the fee structure is different for students. The systems were, and still are, different due to their government funding of further education. Students compete for funded government slots on the basis of ability. Once accepted, they don't transfer institutions without losing their government-funded slot. Many American college students transfer their acceptable credits to other universities. Another important feature was that students weren't required to purchase and carry texts. All textbooks were made available in multiple copies for each class in the library.

Students are enrolled full-time to read, study, and prepare for their coursework, which lasts the entire year. Many U.S. students work part-time jobs, and some may even work full-time by enrolling in fewer courses. Much of this depends on college policies. This wasn't the case in the United Kingdom, as they were full-time students occupying the government-funded slots.

I'm not an expert on British education by any means. I knew it best when I was there and have tried to get some idea of the changes on my several visits back to see old friends. Our best friends were the Scotts, just five houses away in Wollaton, a suburb of Nottingham. Lois and I traveled many weekends with Eileen and Douglas. I'm sure they tired of my many questions about English words and customs. Doug was the Personnel Director for Raleigh Bicycle. They invited us back several times and once for a stay at her brother-in-law's tulip farm for a weekend in Spalding, near Lincoln. We were invited along with their large family and their guests in time for the tulip festival that year. We invited the Scotts to visit us in Florida, and in our home, several times, including for a neighborhood friend's pig roast. Eileen had never drunk a Jell-O shot and drank them like dessert. (Hic!) When Eileen got back to our house, she climbed up our stairs on hands and knees. Doug was a member of Mensa and read a lot of books that we shared and discussed together. On one visit, he told me about discovering Bill Bryson, author of *A Walk in the Wo*ods and other books from one of my favorite authors. I miss Doug and Eileen since they both have passed away.

Bob, before you tell me to take a hike or to get lost, I'm going to take another segue to tell you of the long way of the Appalachian Trail that Bryson writes about. It begins on Spring Mountain, Georgia, and proceeds through twelve states, ending on Mount Katahdin, Maine, a journey of almost 2,200 miles. Bryson refers to his hike along the AT as a trek in the woods. It was made into a hilarious movie in 2015 starring Robert Redford and Nick Nolte. Quite a trek!

To get back on track, Bob, I ran around with Dr. Don Hartley while in England, the sociologist who scheduled and guided me at the Poly. Unfortunately, he died in 2017. I was able to arrange for Don to teach a sociology and a social work course on our campus in 1989–90. He came without June, his wife, that year. He and June became our good friends. Don really knew his stuff, but not much about U.S. plumbing, electricity, and size of restaurant servings.

I arranged for a colleague, Alicia Pieper, to let him use their summer cottage on a lake, with instructions not to pour grease down the drain. The drain plugged. Sewer drainpipes are about six inches in diameter and located on the outside of houses in England. It never normally freezes hard for very long. If you take Ohio (Midwest) weather and cut off the hot and the cold temperatures, you have British weather in Nottingham. They treat Torquay on the southern coast like our Florida, even though it gets cold and the gulf stream flows up to Scotland. They have a few palm trees in the south of England up to the Scotland coast. While visiting there, I observed devout swimmers in the chilly English Channel when the outdoor weather was about 45°F (about 7.3°C). The water temperature was about 59°F (15°C). Brrr! It was convenient to be located in the East Midlands due to the similar distance from coast to coast and from the English Channel to Scotland, with great motorways in between. Other nearby countries included Ireland, France, Germany, and Switzerland. Italy by train is more of a trek, but Nottingham was a great location for travel for Lois and me.

The first thing Don told an advanced social work class at Kent Stark was that he had been teaching for 25 years and given only one "A." He caught on to our system and gave an "A" to a student from another campus within our system. A couple of my good "B" students received "Cs" by his marking and teaching system, even though he tried to adjust to our grading system. Apparently, some British professors/lecturers feel that you must approach their level of knowledge to earn an "A." However, there is a sense of comradery among faculty and students, because classes are broken down to lectures of about 30 or so, seminars of about 15, and tutorials of seven or eight each week for the entire year for each course. At least this was my experience. It became a way to get to know each student better than in the American undergraduate system. Students are required to compete nationally in order to gain entrance to university and/or further education. I felt that this sense of comradery caused many faculty members to think that students were among the more intelligent and that university work was an average C, unless demonstrated otherwise. In the United States, the average grade has often been elevated to a B in many colleges and universities.

The Poly wasn't a residential college like Nottingham University, where I could visit and use the larger library. Lois and I got to know, visit, and hike with our neighbor, Dr. Alan Wint, a chemical engineer, and his wife. He was the Warden (head) of his college at Nottingham University, where he invited me to a high table dinner. It was an honor and I was impressed as I sat and was introduced from the high table platform as a visiting Fulbright Scholar. I have more Nottingham area information and Poly stories, but I'll save the reader at this point.

Yes, Bob, you are now saved!

# CHAPTER VI

## ADDITIONAL AUTHORS

Books deliver information so that experience
has a chance to exercise creativity.
-Richard Diaz

I introduced the reader to some other authors in my
Introductory section. In my early Christian theistic days, I
thought I should read what C.S. Lewis had to say, because
he was one of those authors I'd been introduced to
through his *Scewtape Letters* in my YMCA days working
as an applied Christian. I read *Mere Christianity*. In this
book he combines his radio broadcasts to uplift the spirits
of the British during the bombardments of WW II, and
*The Case for Christianity*, *Christian Behavior* and *Beyond
Personality* in the 1952 edition.

It's a book that makes the case for Christianity in
terms of the basic tenets, regardless of denomination. In
the preface of Mere Christianity, he differentiates between
the formal meaning of Christianity as "belief" and the

casual use of the word as meaning a "good Christian," whereby the word Christian could be left out by the user's extended meaning (Lewis, 1952, pp. 10,11).. He uses the changing meaning and use of the word "gentleman" as an example. Lewis was known for his careful use of words. In this book, he makes the case that we should not get bogged down by the divisions of Greek Orthodoxy, Roman Catholicism, and Protestant, but emphasize the basic beliefs of all Christians. He uses the analogy of a hall in which all Christians are located. The hall leads to many rooms, where the various divisions may go. He states that it's important to be accepting of differences, and that persons be kind and accepting of those Christians who have chosen different rooms or are still waiting in the hall. It's an interesting analogy. If you're a Christian theist who's not limited by the particulars of a specific denomination or faith, I think you'd enjoy the writings of C.S. Lewis. I read him during the time when my skepticism was still within my concept of Christianity. I found the life and background of C.S. Lewis interesting, as a Christian writer who was popular and well-known in Britain and beyond.

He was born in 1898 into a Belfast, Ireland, Protestant family and raised as a Christian. When his mother died from cancer when he was 10, he became upset with God for not granting his prayers. His father never recovered from the loss of his wife to be close to him and his brother. He became more reclusive and an avowed atheist, but over time he became a theist and joined the Anglican Church of England as a Christian in 1929. As a youth, he grew up in a virtual library, filled with books stacked everywhere, and he was free to read whatever he wanted. He was known as Jack by his friends and family. I was impressed with his use of radio broadcasts to rekindle the spirit of the British during the bombarding of England during World War II. I thought he made a good presentation for Christian theists.

The movie, *Shadowlands*, made in 1993 and released in the United States in 1994, emphasized his love and marriage to Joy Davidman in 1956. She died four years later from cancer at age 45. She was the love of his life at age 58. He had never married, and she was 18 years younger. She was a Jewish American poet and writer who was divorced and had two sons. The marriage was criticized by his friend J.R.R. Tolkien. Jack died one week before turning 65 in 1963.

I read the *Screwtape Letters* during my beginning deist stage with Christian leanings. I found it to be an interesting discourse by the satanic Screwtape and Wormwood, who was a lesser devil in training by Screwtape. The letters contain a variety of criticisms and suggestions to Wormwood to help him convert the Christian enemy to satanic ways. In the process, he covers many situations that Christians may experience. The 1961 edition includes a section at the end by Helen Joy Lewis titled "Screwtape Proposes a Toast," stated to be "The wittiest piece … to stimulate the ordinary man to godliness" (Lewis, 1961, Jacket). Later, in this section, Screwtape addresses the annual dinner of the Temptors Training College for young devils in hell. It's a response to Dr. Slubgob, head of devils, as he toasts Screwtape for his success at helping the trainers and Wormwood. Screwtape becomes so upset with Wormwood in his scathing letters that he turns into a large centipede and has to dictate the letter to his secretary, Toadpipe. Apparently, the Christian enemy had fallen in love with the ideal Christian, and Wormwood didn't report this perfect enemy. Screwtape discovered this through the Secret Police (Lewis, 1961, Letter XII). I guess that one has to read it for it to make much sense.

As I recall, it was fun and interesting to read at the time because it was a unique approach. It was assigned reading for my friend when he attended Yale Divinity School as a student in the 1950s. My granddaughter was assigned it in 2013 at a Catholic college.

C.S. Lewis is reported to have enjoyed reading *The Adventures of Tom Sawyer* and *The Adventures of Huckleberry Finn* by Mark Twain and wondered why Samuel Clemens didn't write more stories of this sort. I don't think Jack was able to read *Letters from Earth*, which was reluctantly released by Twain's daughter for publication in 1942, long after Clemens' death in 1910.

I enjoyed Mark Twain's *Letters from Earth* as edited by Bernard DeVoto, *Letter II*. Twain states that humans of all ages place sexual intercourse above all other joys, but sex has no place in heaven. It's replaced by prayer. Secondly, he states that, "In man's heaven, everybody sings!" (Twain, 1963, Letter II p. 17). Even those who didn't sing on earth sing about a dozen hymns most of the day. Thirdly, everyone is playing a harp, in spite of the fact that only a few persons on earth can play one. He says that with all that playing and singing, and with all the noise, it's horrible.

Twain's fourth point is that heaven emphasizes brotherhood, in that all must mix together: "brothers … have to pray together, harp together, Hosannah together—whites, niggers, Jews, everybody. There's no distinction." He goes on to say that "all nations … hate the Jews."(Twain, 1963, pp 16-17) He uses the n-word only twice, as compared to his earlier writings, but his writing is hard on Jews. His fifth and last point regarding the human-contrived heaven deals with the accomplishments of the human intellect, which is quite prodigious here on earth. "And then he contrives a heaven that hasn't a ray of intellectuality in it anywhere!" (Letter II, p. 19). His presentation on how man has imaged heaven provides a good example of his wit and satire. He was a practicing Presbyterian who was probably a deist, but critical of the Bible and church. He was considered to be a liberal for his time, and perhaps still. Obviously, his negative epithets for various peoples cannot be condoned but may have been part of the Zeitgeist at that time.

Previously mentioning Mark Twain's concern for intellectuality, there are several intellectuals on earth that I have admired over the years and to whom Richard Dawkins has made reference. Dawkins clarifies that when he talks of God, he's referring to God as supernatural in the most accepted sense as a personal God. Next, he quotes Einstein, who said, "If something is in me which can be called religious, then it is the unbounded admiration for the structure of the world so far as our science can reveal it" (Dawkins, 2006, p.15). Based on this statement, Dawkins says that Einstein was an atheist. Additionally, I would add that the book about science by Bill Bryson has not only helped to support my extreme agnosticism but adds interesting information on Einstein and his famous E=MC² formula.

Einstein was born in Ulm, Germany, in 1879, and died at Princeton in 1955. He grew up in Munich with little to predict the greatness to follow. He didn't speak until age 3. He eventually moved to Switzerland to attend university. He failed his first entrance exams and entered Zurich Polytechnic Institute to become a high school teacher. He was bright, but not an outstanding student. "His very first paper, *Annalen de Physik,* had to do with the physics of fluids and drinking straws (of all things)" (Bryson, 2006, pp.120-121). In 1905, he produced his famous formula for energy. Bryson points out in his short, illustrated book for children, *A Brief History of Nearly Everything*, that there's enough energy in a walnut to power an entire city and that an average size kid would contain with enough energy in his body to explode with the force of several atomic bombs (Bryson 2003, 2008, p. 64). In his regular edition, Bryson uses the E=MC² formula to state that an average-size adult could potentially produce 7x10 joules of energy to explode the equal of thirty large atomic bombs (Bryson, 2006, p 122). Of course, one would have to know how to release all this energy in both cases. Not only did he explain radiation and space-time, but the last prediction in his general theory of relativity regarding gravitational waves was proven on February 11, 2016, by scientists at the LITGO Lab at Caltech. This was a century after his prediction. Thank heaven he came to the United States in 1933, when Hitler came into power, and became an American citizen at Princeton in 1940. J. Edgar Hoover, who was concerned with his association with socialist and peace organizations, denied his application. Hoover was overruled by the State Department. It was Einstein's letter to President Roosevelt that was responsible for the Manhattan Project.

His gravitational theory proof was used to measure an event in mid-August 2017 and announced on October 17, 2017, when it was published by a variety of sources, including *The Canton Repository* (2017, pp. 1-3) It was described by David Reitze as the most spectacular fireworks in the universe when two neutron stars collided 130 million light years away in the Hydra Constellation. The LITGO researchers alerted astronomers world-wide to focus on the area, which was like looking for a needle in a haystack. Many scientists witnessed the event, reported to be a rare observation of spectacular importance as well as revealing the heavier elements of gold, platinum, and uranium. The Hubble space telescope snapped a picture, revealing the complexity of the cosmic dust from which we are all made. Some of us are able to wear the gold on our fingers and in our teeth as well as platinum rings, if we can afford them.

Yes, Bob, it was a rich discovery that astronomers were able to put their fingers on—thanks to Einstein and LITGO.

Unfortunately, we lost Stephen Hawking, who was another great scientist and world-renown genius, who died in 2018. He was buried in Westminster Abbey next to Sir Isaac Newton. He was sounded out for knighthood in the 1990s but refused as a protest for the lack of funding for science by his government. Hawking, born in 1942, had survived ALS (Lou Gehrig's Disease) since the age of 21. He is known for his position that God and science aren't compatible. Stephen Hawking's final book says there's no possibility of God in our universe (Stephen Hawking, Brief Answers to the Big Questions, 2018).

His mathematics seat was previously occupied by Sir Isaac Newton, 1642–1727. Newton was another genius who had a strange interest in alchemy. He was also interested in the Bible and dissected it carefully to come up with many specific dates, including the Armageddon in 2060. He didn't believe in the Trinity or in Satan. The latter points were considered to be blasphemous, because Christianity was widely accepted at the time in England. These opinions weren't released until 27 years after his death. He would be considered a deist because he said, "Gravity explains the motions of the planets, but it cannot explain who set the planets in motion. God governs all things and knows all that is or can be done" (Achenbach, 2014). Another scientist that many enjoyed and greatly admired was Carl Sagan, who died at the age of 62. Sagan was well respected and well-known for his television series and previous book, *Cosmos*. He includes Newton, among others, as a contributor to modern science. The pictures in this book are fascinating. Since I'm writing and making reference to the Bible, I'll mention that Sagan refers to Job at the beginning of his Chapter 1:

> Have you comprehended the expanse of the earth? Where is the way to the dwelling of light? And where is the place of darkness? (Job 38:18–19, Revised Standard Version)

An interviewer asked Sagan if he thought there was life on other planets. He responded that he thought that life existing beyond our planet was obvious, but when pushed to comment on intelligent life and aliens based on his gut feeling, Sagan said, "I try not to think with my gut. If I am serious about understanding the world, thinking with anything besides my brain, as tempting as that might be, is likely to get me in trouble" (Sagan, 1996, interview). He later said that intelligent life would be so far away, and their knowledge to reach us so advanced, it would be like taking our television and computers to an ant hill and expecting them to comprehend. He said he would wait for the facts of verification before committing himself. He discussed beings (aliens) with advanced brains and intelligence in *Cosmos*, particularly as to how science fiction writers present them. He was highly skeptical of attempts to portray any aliens. I will conclude reference to Sagan with his brief quote: "Science is a way of thinking much more than a body of knowledge" (Sagan, 1995, p. 25). In his book, Sagan devotes chapter four entitled "The Fine Art of Baloney Detection" (Sagan 1995, pp. 201 – 218). whereby he provides tools for skepticism in order to evaluate a variety of beliefs and subjects. A few of his references here include information on UFO's, visitors from outer space, paid endorsements such as the use of tobacco and other products, and many other items that many people hear about and discuss every day with their relatives, neighbors, and friends. I found the chapter a very interesting presentation regarding the use of science for shedding light on the darkness of ignorance as suggested by his subtitle.

While no one can take his place as the original science communicator, it's worthwhile to mention the success, popularity, and recognition of his successor, Neil deGrasse Tyson. He took over the *Cosmos, A Space Time Odyssey (Tyson, 2014)*, a hit science show that popularized science like Sagan did previously. In fact, he credits Sagan for spending time with him as a high school student. He applied to Cornell for undergraduate studies and was impressed with Sagan and his kindness in inviting him to stay overnight with his family if he missed his bus due to the weather. He wanted to emulate Sagan and be the kind of astrophysicist he was. While Sagan wanted to recruit him to attend Cornell, he chose Harvard because he thought there were more resources there to study and pursue astrophysics (Welsh, 2015). He certainly succeeded in becoming an outstanding and well-known promoter of science. With regard to his religion, Tyson says that he is an agnostic and that science and religion cannot be currently reconciled.

Neil deGrasse Tyson published *Astrophysics for People in a Hurry* (Tyson, 2017), which is a delight to read. He presents the complex knowledge of astrophysics in an understandable and humorous way. He tells us that our sun is one of a hundred billion stars in our Milky Way galaxy, which is one of a hundred billion galaxies. He also tells us that there are forty billion planets like earth in the Milky Way. And we think we're all alone! No wonder it's been stated that there are as many stars out there as there are grains of sand on all the beaches and deserts on earth. Wow! You have to read this little book. Just put it down from time to time to reflect on what you've read.

Neil deGrasse Tyson was interviewed by Jane Clayson on *The Point* on NPR on May 2, 2017. In the interview, he said that he went to the planetarium in NYC for his birthday at age 9, which sparked his interest in science. He further stated that the National Academy of Science was started by Abraham Lincoln to advise government in matters of science. Their latest report claims that humans are contributing to the warming of the earth. It's ironic that since 2017 many elected officials deny this and block legislation based on their beliefs; moreover, he points out that humans are made up of the same matter that exist everywhere in our solar system, galaxy, and cosmos. Further, we're all made up of the matter contained in a dog or a tree. We're interconnected in numerous ways with all molecular structures.

Yes, Bob, we can conclude that the pee that the dog deposited on the tree is included. There is much more interesting information in his book.

One Interesting tidbit that he and other scientists touch upon concerns cups of water and breaths of air.

There are enough molecules in a cup of water and a breath of air to equal all the cups of water and all breaths of air that now and ever have been drunk or breathed. That means that every cup of water or breath of air is likely to contain at least one molecule that previously passed through the kidneys or lungs of Jesus, Washington, and even the 911 bombers. Just think of all the possibilities. In his last chapter, Tyson states that the cosmic perspective "is not solely the provenance of the scientist. It belongs to everyone, and he lists ten resultant characteristics of the *cosmic perspective" (Tyson, 2017, pp. 205 – 207)*. Read them!

It's interesting that most outstanding recent scientists declare themselves as agnostics or de facto atheists. Some earlier philosophers put themselves in the same camp. Without extensive listing, I think quickly of Kant and Hume. The latter considered himself to be a skeptic, which leads me to the importance of probability emphasized by Richard Dawkins. He points to an example of Bertrand Russell's celestial teapot. In the parable, he says that a very small teapot (i.e. too small to be seen by a telescope) could be orbiting the sun, and it couldn't be factually disproved. He makes the point that it's not possible to prove or disprove anything. It's possible in mathematics and the natural sciences, but proofs are still based on accepted terms, axioms, and definitions, which are key to the statements of hypotheses and theories.

On the next page, Dawkins introduces us to the preposterous *Flying Spaghetti Monster from the Pastafarianism*, by Bobby Henderson. It's a light-hearted parody on religion, similar to Russell's teapot. U.S. District Judge John

Gerrard rendered a judgment in a lawsuit by a prisoner against the Department of Correctional Services in Lincoln, Nebraska. He said, "This case is different because FSMism as a parody, is designed to look very much like a religion." The prisoner lost his lawsuit (Information from *Lincoln Journal Star*, quoted in *The Canton Repository (Canton Repository 2016).*

Dawkins discusses the probability and existence of God along a seven-point scale he calls " a spectrum of possibilities" accordingly (Dawkins, 2006, pp. 50, 51).

1. Strong theist: 100% probability of God. In the words of C.G. Jung, "I do not believe, I know."
2. De facto theist: Very high probability, but short of 100%. "I cannot know for certain, but I strongly believe in God and live my life on the assumption he is there."
3. Higher than 50%, but not very high. Technically agnostic, but leaning toward theism, "I am very uncertain, but I am inclined to believe in God."
4. Exactly 50%. Completely impartial agnostic. "God's existence and non-existence are exactly equiprobable."
5. Lower than 50%, but not very low. Technically agnostic, but leaning toward atheism. "I don't know whether God exists, but I am included to be skeptical."
6. Very low probability, but short of zero. De facto atheist. "I cannot know for certain, but I think God is very improbable, and I live my life on the assumption that he is not there."

7. Strong atheist: "I know there is no God, with the same conviction as Jung knows there is one."

He adds number seven for symmetry and suggests that one cannot prove that something does not exist. Therefore, he counts himself as a de facto atheist with strong leanings toward his 7th spectrum.

I would have to count myself in the 6th spectrum, along with my wife, as we talked and discussed religion over the years before she died. I think my daughter and son will probably agree, but I can't speak for them. One of the purposes of this presentation is to let readers know my selected thoughts, experiences in my various jobs, and family history. Hopefully others will find this autobiographical journey to be of some interest. Once again, this story is authentic and includes some of the authors and experiences that have influenced my thinking over the years. It's not designed to be an extensive research of books, periodicals, resources, and various authors' contributions with any goals in mind other than those set forth in my Introduction. I do reiterate that it was *The God Delusion* and its author, Richard Dawkins, that motivated me to write this. If a reader wants a more extensive and cogent discourse on religion and agnosticism, they should read *The God Delusion*, as well as the many other scientists and authors I have included.

Bob, my purpose is not to proselytize anyone with my views. It's just to reveal my journey. I don't need to convert you, anyway.

Before I leave the discussion of additional authors, I ran across a paper by Daniel Septimus titled, *Must a Jew Believe in God?* The article was given to me by friend and neighbor, Neal Libster. Neal and I met in the late 1960s as part of the Civil Rights Commission studying the city of Canton as part one of four national projects. He was selected as a builder of low-cost housing in the black community. I'd recently served as director of Mrs. Timken's pilot project at Lathrop School and resulting community schools.

As I walk past Neal's house with my dog, I usually stop and sit on his stoop to talk over old times and many other topics, including my agnosticism. One day he handed me the article by Daniel Septimus, which he had received as part of a discussion at Temple Israel in Canton. Septimus traces the importance of God in Judaism from the ancient world through modernity to secular humanist Jews. Interestingly, he uses CE (common era) instead of AD (anno domini) to avoid the Christian bias that Prothero avoids in his book, *God Is Not One,* discussed later. He does the same in his references, including BCE (before common era) and CE.

Septimus says that Atheism and agnosticism only emerged as real options in the modern era, as a consequence of separation of church and state, and above all, the reliance on science for explanations of natural phenomena.

He quotes Erich Fromm, who states in his interpretation of the Hebrew Bible: "…one who does not believe in God can still come very close to living a life that is Jewish in Spirit." (Septimus, 2018?) * He continues with another quote from Howard Wettstein, philosopher at the University of California, Riverside, who emphasizes awe over belief in his book, *Awe and Religious Life*. Septimus tells of the secular humanist Jews who think that belief in God devalues humans. Finally, after his two-page discussion, he asks, "So, must a Jew believe in God?" He answers, "It depends on how you define four words, 'must,' 'Jew,' 'believe,' and of course, 'God.' In short: probably. And probably not."(Septimus, 2018?, Conclusion)*

> *Thearticle was referred to me by Rabbi Jon Adland in 2018 from My Jewish Learning after he introduced it for discussion at the Temple. I found no date of publication on the webcite.)

I found the Septimus article about God in Judaism interesting. Obviously, I'm not an authority on Judaism, or any religion for that matter. I merely attempt to paraphrase and quote from parts of Septimus' paper that I found very interesting,

# CHAPTER VII

## MORE INFORMATION

Information is not knowledge.
-Albert Einstein

A few years ago, a friend from church knew that I expressed agnostic views, so he dropped off a book to reveal his view of gaps, with a note saying I might find it interesting to read. The book was *The Reason for God: Belief in an Age of Skepticism* by Timothy Keller, pastor of Redeemer Presbyterian Church in New York City, located in the inner city. He states that he has nearly 6,000 attendees at five services. I can see that his church has value for his inner-city members, which he says represents some members with Ivy League degrees. His examples consist of people with crises of health and death, whereby faith in God grants comfort and acceptance for those boxed in or influenced by circumstances and location.

Richard Dawkins deals with gap phenomenon in his last chapter of *The God Delusion* when he cites *Binker* by

A.A. Milne and presents his poem, "Now We Are Six".
He includes Binker as an example of adult theistic beliefs.
Milne's books, including *Winnie the Pooh*, were great
readers for our children. I found the poem in my daughter's book and include it here, using Dawkins shorter
format, because I think the poem is so great. It almost
brings tears to my eyes.

> Binker—what I call him—is a secret of
>    my own
> And Binker is the reason why I never
>    feel alone
> Playing in the nursery, sitting on the stair,
> Whatever I am busy at, Binker will be there,
> Oh, Daddy is clever, He's a clever sort of man,
> And Mummy is the best since the
>    world began
> And Nanny is Nanny, and I call her Nan –
> But they can't see Binker.
> Binker's always talking, 'cos I'm teaching him
>    how to speak
> He sometimes likes to do it in a funny sort
>    of squeak,
> And he sometimes likes to do it in a hoodling
>    sort of roar. . .
> And I have to do it for him 'cos his throat is
>    rather sore.
> Oh Daddy is clever, he's a clever sort of man,
> And Mommy knows all that anybody can,
> And Nanny is Nanny, and I call her Nan—

But they don't know Binker.

Binker's brave as lions when we're running in
the park;

Binker's brave as tigers when we're lying in
the dark;

Binker's brave as elephants. He never, never
cries . . .

Except (like other people) when the soap
gets in his eyes.

Oh, Daddy is Daddy, he's a Daddy sort
of man,

And Mummy is as Mummy as anybody can,

And Nanny is Nanny, and I call her Nan . . .

But they're not like Binker.

Binker is not greedy, but he likes things to eat,

So, I have to say to people when they're
giving me a sweet,

"Oh, Binker wants a chocolate, so could you
give me two?"

And then I eat it for him, 'cos his teeth are
rather new.

Well, I'm very fond of Daddy, but he doesn't
have time to play,

And I'm very fond of Mummy, but she some-
times goes away,

And I'm often cross with Nanny when she
wants to brush my hair . . .

But Binker is always Binker and is certain to
be there (Dawkins, 2008, p. 348)

For those who have the need, and are boxed in by social-ization or by the need to think within that need (i.e. inabil-ity to think beyond that box), and for those who Dawkins says are educated and rational thinkers, we may come back to psychological and/or psychiatric needs, much like a Binker for adults. Anyhow, I see that religion may serve a need for some people. Is it trite to bring up the old saying, "You don't find atheists in the foxholes," or the statement that "a scientist does not believe it until he sees it," and "the non-scientist does not see it until he believes it"? I would have been more receptive to Timothy Keller's book when I was a YMCA director. While I can understand some people's need to fill the gap, I can't bridge the faith required now to convert me after my years of increasing agnosticism based on science, rational thinking, and probability. Yes, I do remember that I previously included Dawkin's sugges-tion that one cannot prove that God doesn't exist.

In his book about science, Bill Bryson states that our human body has ten thousand trillion cells, which are the same cells that make up all matter. Since all molecules exist-ing outside our bodies are the same as the molecules that make up my body, I believe that when I die, my molecules will survive and continue to make up other structures; there-fore, I shall be cremated so that my molecular ashes will take up less space from the more enjoyable bucolic scenery. (This conforms with Neil deGrasse Tyson's interview.)

I want to add another book that I'd heard about but never read until recently, *God is Not One* by Stephen Prothero. He does a good job of describing Islam, Christianity, Confucianism, Hinduism, Buddhism,

Yoruba religion, Judaism, Daoism, and last chapter A Brief Coda on Atheism. I didn't read it when it first came out because I thought I knew enough about each religion. I was wrong and recommend it to all who may be curious, or just want to be informed about different religions.

The last section is on atheists, which includes some extreme agnostics, such as Richard Dawkins. Prothero lumps Dawkins, Dennett, Harris, and Hitchens together as "the 'Four Horseman' of the angry atheist apocalypse" (Prothero, 2010, p. 28). Since Dawkins was the primary impetus to write my journey, I have found him to be informative and interesting with his factual revelations of cruel fanaticisms, but I didn't find him angry in my reading of *The God Delusion*. While Dawkins' book is geared to proselytize, it was his rational and scientific approach that appealed to me, along with his extensive research and style of writing.

I did like the section by Prothero on "Friendly Atheists" where he mentions William Lobdell, a former religion writer for *The Los Angeles Times*, who tells of his journey from evangelism to Catholicism to atheism (Prothero, p. 327) Like my odyssey, it's the description of his journey without any attempt to convert others to his point of view. He refers to a public comment by Christopher Hitchens about the death of Jerry Falwell: 'if you gave Falwell an enema, he could be buried in a matchbox.' (Prothero, 2010, p. 320). I thought it could be a humorous wisecrack that could be modified to include anyone who thought another person was full of it. It need not to be about burial after death, or even about Jerry Falwell.

I haven't listed all the readings, books, authors, and articles I encountered during my years of taking and teaching courses, or all the other reading I've done to this date. I have selected a few as benchmarks to describe my journey of being a Christian during my earlier years to my evolution to an agnostic. Any one of the authors referenced have written books and articles that would take years for a person to read. Having said that, if I've touched on any authors or books that pique your curiosity, try to delve into their writings, as well as their references. As Albert Einstein said, "Once you stop learning you start dying."

# BELL TELEPHONE EXPERIMENT

While I've read mostly non-fiction, I believe there's much to be learned from fiction novels, plays, and poetry. Very early on I ran across a book emphasizing the importance of fiction entitled, *Toward the Liberally Educated Executive* by the Fund for Adult Education. The book had two editors and fifteen well-known contributors who were CEOs and academics. They searched for seventeen promising young men from middle management levels from all the Bell Telephone systems at that time. They were selected by W.D. Gillen, President of the Bell Telephone Company of Pennsylvania. He was a trustee of the University of Pennsylvania and wanted to expand the education and broaden the point of view of these selected future CEOs. They were to spend nine months of extensive study of a liberal arts curriculum directed by Dr. Morse Peckham, Associate Professor of English, the University of Pennsylvania. This was to help these college graduates overcome their "trained incapacity" by their specialization. Mr. Gillen thought that managers needed perspectives for management decisions helped by a wider intellectual experience. They were each granted a ten month leave of absence with full salary.

The students were often exasperated by their introduction to early oriental history and learning about *The Tale of Genji*. Apparently, the study of James Joyce's *Ulysses* was the most controversial part of the curriculum, as they learned about Bloom's day in Dublin on June 16, 1904. The Ulysses course included a "pony" literature on Joyce, dictionaries of mythology, encyclopedias, and Webster, as each man had to prepare one or more reports for his seminar group. The first nine months included 550 hours of lectures, discussions, and seminars. The final four weeks were set aside for students to read on their own.

One accountant, who was also a musician, initially thought that *Ulysses* was a waste of time. He volunteered to report on Chapter 11, the "Sirens" section. The report was so thorough that the professor had it copied for distribution to the whole seminar and for the use of his future graduate students. I have to include that the professor invited 160 of America's leading intellectuals, including Lewis Mumford, Clyde Kluckhohn, W.N. Alden, Jacques Lipchitz, Delmore Schwartz, Henry S. Commager, Virgil Thompson and Eric Goldman. I read this book soon after receiving my Master of Arts degree in 1958, so it was one of my favorites. Most of the above guest lecturers were included in my studies at that time.

At this point as a significant segue, I include information about a very important friend who, in my opinion, represents the kind of former executive from the Bell Telephone Company that W.D. Gillen's program at the University of Pennsylvania was designed to service. Guermo (Bill) Acosta is unique in the fact that he received extensive educational preparation as a youth, and by his own later inspiration and drive. I met Bill on Marco Island in 2014 and interviewed him in 2018. He is Jewish, with a Catholic mother, and attended services of both religions with different family members.

He was an immigrant from Columbia.

He was born in 1933 in Barranquilla, Columbia, which was a cosmopolitan city with a variety of international enclaves. His father, Benigno, was Columbia's diplomatic representative to the United Nations. The house was filled with books on literature, philosophy, and the arts, which were discussed during family dinner. His mother was Josephine Carbonell, a well-known family name in Columbia. They sent Bill to the German school where he learned to speak German. Later the Catholic school was taken over by the French, whereupon he studied and learned French and English. After high school, he enrolled in the University of the Andes, which emphasized academics, classics, philosophy, and literature. He said it was an international faculty and included further study at the University of Illinois in Champaign.

No, Bob, the city … sorry to bust your bubble. Let's cork it for now and move on.

Bill earned two degrees at U of I, one in Mechanical Engineering, and one in Electrical Engineering. He moved to Columbus, Ohio, with the Western Electric Company, where he was able to enroll at Ohio State and receive a Master's Degree in Control Engineering. While in Columbus, he enrolled in Ohio Dominican College to study economics and finance and became one of the founders of the Western Electric International Company, which ultimately became AT&T International. Bill was named President of AT&T Brazil, the headquarters for developing AT&T operations for South America from Mexico to Brazil. He recruited managers for the AT&T operations in South America. (see picture)

*- Bill Acosta beside his company-assigned personal jet.*

As I look over his preparation from his childhood education through adulthood, and his accomplishments and responsibilities as a CEO over South America, I see that he greatly supersedes W.D. Gillen's program for CEOs at the University of Pennsylvania. The reader should know that Guermo (Bill) Acosta speaks very highly of the opportunities made to him as an immigrant, and to all Americans. He certainly was a company devotee when he said, "I saw the Bell system to be like a gigantic octopus with tentacles that covered a multitude of businesses and research activities for the benefit of the country." (Acosta, 2018, interview). This statement reminds me of Charles E. Wilson's famous statement as Secretary of Defense under President Eisenhower: "What's good for General Motors, is good for the country." If you didn't know, he was the former President and Chairman of the Board of General Motors.

Okay, Bob, let's shift gears to an example of religion gone awry and some other unusual religious beliefs.

I add this section to comment on some unusual thoughts, ideas, and beliefs that aren't part of my journey from a Christian theist to a current agnostic. The extraterrestrial influence and conspiracy theories aren't harmful or dangerous to other lives; however, Jon Krakauer's nonfiction book resulted in the loss of life. The book deals with two brothers who insisted that they received a commandment from God to kill their sister-in-law and her child for no other reason than unyielding faith. Occasionally, these kinds of stories show up and are considered to be messianic delusions with tragic consequences. The book is titled *Under the Banner of Heaven: A Story of Violent Faith* and fits as an extreme example of Dawkin's comments on the dangers of religion.

I first deal with stories closest to home and then follow with another experience I had while teaching a youth Sunday school class at my Presbyterian church during the 1970s. I'll start with stories about a friend, followed by a family experience.

Bob, I have a good friend who's retired from being an engineer with management responsibilities at a major corporation. I mention this to reveal that he's an educated and accomplished person who adheres to the writings of Erich von Daniken, who wrote *Chariots of the Gods*. This was a *New York Times* best seller in 1968. It was followed by several popular books about the influence on our earthly culture of extra-terrestrial astronauts several thousand years ago. He backs up his hypothesis with pictures of phenomena and designs that can only be seen from on high. He interprets these pictures and designs as being provided only by extra-terrestrial beings with their superior knowledge.

While many things are possible, many things are improbable. I see that he is listed as a non-fiction writer. Apparently, this is due to his gathering and presentation of facts to support his hypothesis. I would classify his writing and interpretations in videos and lectures as science fiction. I keep repeating: the scientist believes it when he sees it; the nonscientist sees it when he believes it. For this reason, most scientists and academics disagree with his interpretations and hypothesis. I must add however, that an issue of The Week magazine, (June 14 2019, p. 16), quotes an article by Helene Cooper in the New York Times. The article reports that the Pentagon is urging pilots to take UFO's seriously by reporting all details.

Bob, don't disappear quickly, but you said that Daniken's hypothesis sounds like a true story that he made up. What you mean by that contradiction is that you have looked over von Daniken's book, lectures, and video presentations. He provides extensive information from the Bible and archeological drawings, carvings and petroglyphs, and aerial photographs as facts to corroborate his hypothesis. While the information he presents is factual, his interpretation of these facts cannot be corroborated. He conducts an extensive review and discussion of these facts to lend credence to his hypothesis of the previous influence of terrestrial cosmonauts. He includes support by a Russian scientist, and more recently by Russian Professor Buzhich. Carl Sagan refutes much of this in his 1995 book.

My friend believes that these paleo-contacts by God are to reveal Christianity to earthlings in order to guide us and correct our errant way. He also believes in Darwin's theory of evolution. This starts with genus homo and evolves to biblical times, when Jesus was sent to lead us humans. He includes the story of the virgin birth of Christ as being true due to the advanced knowledge of the past alien visitors. In other words, they were able to produce the Virgin Mary story in order to provide a credible biblical account.

Bob, I don't think that my friend is a "Lone Ranger." I discovered that there's a lot of information available on this subject. Many people believe that UFOs are occupied today by extra-terrestrials beings. Further, some conspiracy theories suggest that the information of occupants and their spacecraft is known to the U.S. government, but the government is protecting our citizens by keeping it secret. Sagan questions and refutes the above in his 1995 book. Some of these believers are known to be educated and presumed to be intelligent. Wow!

Wait, Bob, you may feel like a broken dumb waiter as you don't have believable information to elevate your knowledge.

My brother Ollie and teenage nephew Todd told me once that they observed a UFO in the sky that took off rapidly and disappeared. They both observed it and swear by it. They said they weren't smoking any funny stuff. Additionally, another nephew, David, in Florida, is an adherent of Daniken's theory and believes that the government knows all the UFO alien information, including the whereabouts of their spaceships, but is withholding this information to protect us from "flipping out." He told me there's a lot of credible information available. There are numerous adherents to these kinds of beliefs—more than believe in the Flying Spaghetti Monster. Yes, UFOs exist. They are just unidentified flying objects.

Bob, I did google the FSM and found some digestible information that I will regurgitate to you.

To digest many ideas and presentations in order to make some sense out of FSMism, one idea may be worthy of comment. They say their religion doesn't actually expect followers to believe in their history and teachings. They state that since many Christians don't actually believe their history and beliefs as presented in their Christian Bible and churches. Their idea is to acknowledge this disbelief within religion. However, if a person joins FSM, they can become a minister by paying $25. I wonder if this includes some kind of tax exemption? While I find this interesting, I join in with scientists and academics who don't agree with FSMism.

Sorry, Bob, you can't join either. Don't ask me how I know, but you're an agnostic.

Since it was my brother Ollie who opened my eyes to agnosticism, I feel that the reader may enjoy this segue on his outlook or philosophy about money, which he shared with his wife, Fran. Yes, Bob, it was *Kukla, Fran and Ollie*, without Kukla (no clowning). For those of you who are too young to know, *Kukla, Fran and Ollie* was a popular, award-winning TV show that ran from 1947 to 1957. Ollie was a single-toothed dragon, and Kukla was a clown devised by puppeteer Burr Tillstrom. Fran was a popular singer and comedian who held the show together. It made headlines in the 1950s from support by some of America's most famous people.

Ollie and Fran lived "high on the hog." They owned a villa in Acapulco with three MDs, where they went for two weeks every ten weeks. They owned three expensive places in southern Florida in sequence. They frequently traveled abroad.

When I was on my Fulbright with Lois in Nottingham, they flew over to visit via the Concorde and returned on the QE2. We visited them in The Villages where Fran died, and Ollie returned to Naples, Florida. When I visited him in Naples in 2016 before he died, he was in the Lely Palms Manor Care Nursing Home. He died there on Medicaid. He told me, "I lived high and spent all my money. I'm glad I did. Fran and I enjoyed every bit of it." He provided for son Todd, who was unemployed after an accident. He also invited James, from Ohio, to live with him in Florida after James had two strokes. James died in Akron, Ohio, in 2018 at the age of 60. It's sad to see another bright, younger nephew join the cosmic dust.

# CHAPTER VIII

## SUMMARY AND CONCLUSION

Nothing is worth more than this day
-Johann Wolfgang Von Goethe

I indicated in The Introduction a few of the topics and authors I'd be writing about as a Christian by culture through my stages of religiosity and agnosticism within my broadly stated goals. It all fits within non-fiction, except for the creation of the communication and responses with Bob, who is known as Paul Indrome. I chose Bob with the idea that I could use and accuse him for all those terrible puns. You can see that I just wasn't able to keep him under control. Most of his puns were blatant, but there were a couple that were a little more subtle. I'm aware that my idea to use communications with Bob surely lacks the wit, humor, ability, and clever subject matter used by C.S. Lewis and Samuel Clemens' Mark Twain in their use of letters. My aha! moment may have turned into a ha - ha, or laughable, result.

The main motivation to undertake this endeavor was Richard Dawkin's book *The God Delusion*. Not only have I extensively learned from, and leaned on, his writings, but I've drawn on other authors, including Wells, and other famous scientists. My goals are much more limited and tied in with my autobiographical journey, which includes other professional jobs and experiences.

The reader may be surprised to know that I still enjoy attending the Presbyterian church, where I joined as a charter member during my YMCA days when I moved to the Canton area. It's a venue where I can still meet and talk with old friends that I may not see otherwise. Obviously, I like to attend on those Sundays when there's a coffee hour after the service. If mere acquaintances should happen to read this information, they will disapprove of my presentation; however, good friends may not agree with my ultimate position, but they won't ostracize me, as will many of my lesser- known members of the congregation. After all, one would not likely find many persons admitting to agnosticisms on the church roll. I don't expect that most, if any, will be attracted to this writing. This is just MY journey!

Earlier I said that I'd return to the discussion of creeds. The two major creeds in Christianity are the Nicene Creed and the Apostles' Creed. They both state that God had only one son, Jesus Christ, who was born of the Virgin Mary. Both creeds emphasize the Trinity, which includes the Father, Son, and Holy Spirit. They state that

Jesus was crucified by Pontius Pilate and suffered as a human. He was dead, buried, and arose from the dead on the third day, from whence he will return to judge the quick and dead, who are believers. The non-believers will not be saved and will go to hell. Thereafter, Jesus will rule the world in peace. Two additional key beliefs include the resurrection of the body after death, and the importance of the forgiveness of sins. Some Christians into eschatology believe in the Rapture implied by the creeds but not emphasized by all as a separate term. Wikipedia refers to the Rapture as a belief in the second coming of Jesus to earth, whereby Jesus appears in the sky and raises all believers who have accepted Christ up into Heaven. All others will go to hell. Some Christian denominations greatly emphasize the Rapture. I've never heard the term used in my church. I was surprised to be asked by one of my former employees if I believed in the Rapture. After I listened to his explanation, he was surprised that I didn't know about the importance of the term as emphasized by his church, but not mentioned as such by my church.

The Rapture discussion occurred about 1975, by which time my agnosticism was developing, and the idea seemed very questionable, or as Bob might say, "a pie in the sky" concept. I can understand those theists and deists who feel that God fills a needed gap via belief, as referred to by Richard Dawkins when he discusses gaps. He states that gaps are liked by creationists and scientists alike, but for quite different reasons. His discussion refers to gaps in knowledge or understanding, whereby creationists believe that any ignorance goes back, by default, to God being the answer to all imponderable questions. Scientists, on the other hand, see lack of knowledge as a challenge to do further research to find an answer. The idea that the scientist doesn't believe it until he sees it, and the non-scientist doesn't see it until he believes it, is very appropriate here.

Bob, you say that eschatology sounds like some sort of scatology, and I know you're using the term humorously, but except for your inclusion of (corny?) puns, my overall goal is a more serious presentation of my journal and autobiographic experience as I have progressed through my various stages of religion to arrive at my Ptolemaic view of Jesus.

# THE PTOLEMAIC VIEW
# OF CHRISTIANITY

In the non-scientific realm of early philosophy after Aristotle, Claudius Ptolemy developed his view of the sun revolving around the earth. We know now that our solar system is heliocentric, and that the earth revolves around the sun, as proved by Nicolaus Copernicus. I maintain that the Son revolves around the earth for most religions, including the Christian perspective. Bob, I know it's a pun, but let me explain. It goes all the way back to Zoroastrianism and its beliefs that are all based on the earth and afterlife on earth. Zarathrusta will return to earth after his death to rule in peace, followed by his sons returning to earth to rule forever.

The Old Testament of the Christian Bible deals with God's treatment of non-believers, conflicts, wars, punishments, and prophecies for earth, as well as God's return to earth via a messiah. The New Testament states that God sent his only son, Jesus Christ, to earth, as described in the Nicene Creed and Apostles' Creed. He became human and suffered until death, whereupon He rose up to heaven. All references in Christianity deal with human life on earth, or pertain to the earth's surrounding space, known as heaven, as well as a place we go after death. People refer to heaven as up. Now, if I'm in Australia, heaven is still up, which would be down from the United States. So, if heaven exists, it must be out there someplace. Therefore, the story of the Son of God revolves around the earth. This is my idea of the Ptolemaic view of Christianity. I realize that the Son revolving around the earth is the aforementioned pun on Ptolemy's view of the sun revolving around the earth. We know that his view of the sun and earth was refuted. My concept of Christ, the Son of God, may also be questioned by extreme agnostics. Since Ptolemy's view of the sun revolving around the earth has been refuted, I have suggested that Christ the Son may also be questioned, or even refuted by science.

Since Christians believe God is creator of heaven and earth, let's explore what science has revealed about the vastness of this creation. Carl Sagan estimated that the number of planets in the universe to be 10 billion trillion, and planet earth is one of these. Sagan said that the nearest planet to our nearest star in our Milky Way is two (2) light years away. In 2016, planet Proximba was discovered in the habital zone of Proxima Centauri, the closest star to earth.

Our Christian belief includes a personal God to whom we can pray and receive answers and/or guidance in return. While many things are possible, some might say anything is possible. This means that God is very busy and has selected only planet earth for Christianity. Other religions are based on the behavior of earthlings or their after-life. Dawkins raises the subject of improbability in his Chapter 3, "Arguments for God's Existence," where he raises the question, "Who made God?" He answers the question in his Chapter 4. Without going into the kind of detail that he describes, I'll share a shorter explanation. Rather than God creating man in his own image, as stated in Genesis 1:27, I suggest that man has created God according to his own image and needs. This idea goes back to the God of the Old Testament with his human emotions. This was first suggested to me by H.L. Menken's book. The New Testament is centered around the human quality of Jesus to suffer, and his concern to look after the welfare of all humans on earth. I think the story of the Good Samaritan is an excellent example of the last point. Has man created God to meet his own needs? I think so! A scientific study reported in *USA Today* by Doug Stanglin discusses the proceedings of The National Academy of Science, which referred to the values of man being imputed to God. The report was based on the study of values. I did not see the study.

Readers may wonder if I've ever revealed any of my positions while teaching my classes. The texts I've used for the introductory course have included religion and a lot of other topics. Sociology is areligious and presents empirical evidence as part of the scientific process. Sociologists are not theologians and don't have the tools to evaluate beliefs. We can only reveal the history, location of religions, and their demographic data, as well as attitudinal studies. The demographic information is always changing and not easy to accurately present. When I presented my master's thesis in 1958, I reported that there were 268 religious bodies in the United States. The 2010 Census reveals 236 religious groups. Actually, there were about 40,000 religious organizations in the world in 2017. Of course, definitions of religious bodies, groups, and organizations differ. Additionally, there have been amalgamations of denomination in the United States. I'm sure that many have conducted attitudinal surveys and would disagree with my presentation and conclusions. I've already included several examples of viewpoints with which I have disagreed as part of my presentation. Let me introduce (and steal) a witty paradox by Karen Owens, referenced by Dawkins (2006, p. 78).

> Can omniscient God, who
> Knows the future, find
> The omnipotence to
> Change His future mind

Isn't that an interesting thought?

Some readers may think it ironic that I continue to attend church, or that some of my best old friends and idols were ordained ministers. My YMCA camp leaders included my earliest idol, Dale "Zeke" Turner, followed by my YMCA experience in Wilmington, Delaware under Henry Kohl Executive Secretary, and the divinity graduates, including Parker Lansdale, Frank Mullen, and Fred Hanna. They and Zeke Turner were all important relationships for me. The Wilmington YMCA goup included our wives. I have continued to meet yearly with Don Andrews from Texas, who was my former pastor many years ago. He may not travel back this year. We all are/ or were just old friends. I also support the work of my current pastor, Dr. Rich Holmes, who fulfills the needs of those who need to believe in belief. Yes, Yale Divinity School graduates played an important role in my life. Of course, they would accept me, but disagree with my agnostic belief.

I'm getting near to bringing this presentation of my life experiences and agnostic thoughts to a close by using this saying by Emily Dickinson:

> That it will never come again
> Is what makes life so sweet.

Dawkins includes this saying as he discusses inspiration. Mark Twain's reference to the kind of heaven that man has contrived for himself is not a very desirable kind of place. Remember what he said? His satirical account is replaced by the Christian belief that heaven is a very desirable and peaceful place for those who make it there. We will all be received in the arms of Jesus and be reunited with our parents and friends who faithfully followed this same belief and were admitted. If we accept Jesus, we're granted eternal life.

Science would suggest that life is made up of the same cosmic dust that's been around for billions and billions of years. Scientists say that when we die, our atoms continue to exist forever. Mark Twain stated that he didn't fear death because he didn't exist for billions of years and it didn't bother him one bit. I think many of us don't fear death but are apprehensive about the process of dying. I wonder why it's so difficult to alleviate suffering for those who are terminally ill and don't want to suffer, not to mention suffering from all causes.

Bob, when you say, "that's the spirit," I take it that you mean I'm taking a positive attitude. However, this fits in with the Native American concept that their burial sites are hallowed grounds. Christians, however, construe your comment to mean that there's a spirit that continues forever in Heaven. In 1901 an experiment was conducted on six dying patients by Dr. Duncan MacDougal to prove that the human soul had mass and was measurable, which he determined to weigh a specific number of grams. The experiment was covered on TV in 2010 as part of *Historic Mysteries* as the 21 Gram Theory. This aroused some interest. We know the body will lose weight upon death. After all, oxygen and air are not weightless. Is there a soul that can be measured? My rational thinking cap suggests that it doesn't exist, which further leads to my agnosticism. Once again, I restate that I am a social scientist who adheres to the methods of science. As I approach the end of this presentation, I reflect on the end of my journey and Erik Erikson's Eight stages of life (Erikson, 1963, pp. 247 -274). The last stage is Ego Integrity VS. Despair (Erikson, 1963, pp. 268-9). According to Erikson, at this last stage a person looks back over their life as a life of success and fully integrated in maturity, or does a person look back over his/her life as missed opportunities and failures? It is too late to make amends, or to do over again.

I feel very fortunate to have married a wonderful wife, with wonderful children, and many wonderful friends who may not agree at all with my position.

The end ... Oops!, Bob asked me to end on a more humorous vein, (or should I *say,*vain ?) Bob says that Walter Matthau's wife (Carol) asked Walter if he had any final arrangements that he'd like to make at the time of his death. Walter said, "Surprise me!"

P.S. I would like to emulate my grandfather, Marquis D. Cring, as a newspaper publisher and college recruiter by contributing all profits of this publication to the Stark Campus Scholarship Fund to help students attain their goals.

# ACKNOWLEDGEMENTS

I must acknowledge the many scientists and authors that I have selected as being influential for my religious journey. They are cited in the text as referenced. I am indebted to colleague Dr. Jayne Moneysmith, Professor of English, who provided valuable suggestions and editing for my first manuscript. She recommended that I exclude reference to Paul (Bob) Indrome to see how it read. I included Bob as an enabler for my puns that the reader had to endure. Also, my secretary, Sharon Schreffler played a key role in communicating with Dr. Moneysmith and my son Rick Worrell.

Sharon was valuable for deciphering my handwriting. She contributed much time beyond the small remuneration that she received. Many staff were helpful, including Ellen and Jeanne, in the steno office of Kent State.

Additionally, my son provided much initial typing, computer assistance, and promotional ideas through his business, Worrell Advertising Agency. Neighbors Bill Kalkreuth, a psychologist, and Kit Lupsor, an artist, were helpful. Bill prodded me by continually asking about my progress and Kit provided me with the Prothero book which I needed.

Of course, many staff at FriesenPress were very helpful along the way. Particularly, My Team of Ari, Diane and Jacob, who provided great assistance to publish and bring my book to fruition. Jacob returned many helpful phone calls and provided the cover design picture that I selected.

I really appreciate all the assistance and help along the way as Forest Gump said, "That is all I got to say about that."

# REFERENCES

Achenbach, J. (July 10, 2014). Washington D.C.: Washington Post.
Apostle's Creed and Nicene Creed provided by Northminster Presbyterian Church.

Bryson, B. (2006). *A Short History of Nearly Everything.* New York: Broadway Books. This is a book revealing extensive information on science.

Bryson, B. (1990). *The Mother Tongue.* New York: William Morris & Co.

Bryson, B. (1958). *A Walk in the Woods.* New York: Broadway Books.
Note: It was also made into a movie starring Robert Redford, Nick Nolte, and Emma Thompson, 2015. Broad Green Pictures: Los Angeles, CA.

Bryson, B. (2003-2008). *A Really Short History of Nearly Everything.* New York: Random House, Children's Book Division.

Chaucer, G. (1387-4000). *The Canterbury Tales.* While I reference this, I have not read his 24 stories. It covers 1700 lines in Medieval English.

Crossan, J.D. (1991). *The Historical Jesus: The Life of a Mediterranean Jewish Peasant.* San Francisco: Harper & Row, a division of Harper Collins.

Crossan, J.D. (1988). *The Cross that Spoke.* New York: Harper & Row.
This is cited as an award winning book. I did not read.

Dawkins, R. (2006). *The God Delusion.* London, England: Bantam Books. The paperback edition was published by First Mariner Books in 2008.

Einstein, A. (1905). *Annalen der Physik,* was a scientific journal. This was his first published paper. This account was referenced by Bryson, B. (2006). *A Short Story of Nearly Everything.* Published in Germany by the Economic Geology Publishing Co.

Erikson, E.N. (1963, 2nd ed.). *Childhood and Society. New York: W.W.* Norton & Co. Chapter 7 has *Eight Ages of Man*, p. 149-174.

*Five Gospels,* synopsis of report. (December 27, 1993). The Canton Repository: Canton OH.

Goethe, J. (2016). *Nothing is Worth More Than this Day.* New York: Workman Publishing.

Henderson, B. (2006). *Flying Spaghetti Monster from the Pastafariaism.* New York: Villard Books. Villard Books is a division of Random House.

Hertz, P. (1999). *Zorastrianism: World Religions.* Langhorn, PA: Chelsea House Publishers. This is one of a series she wrote for World Religions. She was a former school teacher.

*Historic Mysteries. (2010).* NBC: New York, filmed in Memphis, TN. It was made into a film starring Sean Penn, produced by This Is That Productions, 2003.

*Is God Dead?* (April 8, 1966). *Time Magazine* cover. New York: Time Warner.

Kagawa, Toyohiko. Japanese poet. http://en.em.wikipedia.org.
Note: He was referred to as the St. Francis of Japan.

Keller, T. (2003). *The Reason for God: Belief in an Age of Skepticism.* New York: Riverhead Books.

Keller, W. (1957). *The Bible as History.* New York: William Morrow & Son.
Also a revised paperback edition with post script by Joachim Rehork, Harper Collins, 2015.

Kilpatrick, J.J. (1946). *The Writer's Art.* Kansas City & New York: Andrews, McMeel & Parker.

Kirkpatrick, C. (1949). (1949). *Religion and Humanitarianism: A Study of Institutional Implications.* APA Washington, D.C.: Psychological Monographs.

Krakauer, J. (2003-2004). *Under the Banner of Heaven: A Story of Violent Faith.* New York: Anchor Books, a division of Random House.

Lewis, C.S. (2001). *The Screwtape Letters.*, and Lewis, H.J. (1959). *Screwtape Proposes a Toast.* New York: Harper & Row, 1962. While the dates are listed separately, the title and publication date of 1962 contains both.
Lewis, C.S. (1952, ed.). *Mere Christianity.* New York: MacMillan.

Lewis, C.S. (1943). *The Case for Christianity.* New York: MacMillan.

Lewis, C.S. (1943). *Christian Behavior.* New York: MacMillan.

Lewis, C.S. (1943). *Beyond Personality.* New York: MacMillan.

Ling, J. (2001). *The Physics Handbook.* New York: McGraw Hill Book Co.

LITGO Lab at Caltech (http://www.theverge.com (see David Reitzer)

Mel Brooks, director. (1981). *The History of the World*. A movie from 20th Century Fox, Los Angeles.

Mencken, H. (1930, revised 1946). *Treatise on the Gods*. New York: Alfred A. Knopf, Inc.

Milne, A.A. (1927). *Now We Are Six*. London, England: Methuen & Co.
My children remember his publication of *Winnie the Pooh*.

Morgan Freeman interview on WKSU, April 3, 2016.
This was an interesting interview conveyed by his conversation with Jane Clayson.

Mosberger, D. (September 25, 2014). *Huffington Post or Huff Post*.

Mullen, T. (2001). *A Very Good Marriage*. Richmond, IN: Friends United Press.
This is a description of his wife's death from cancer.

Pellegrino, J. (1994). *Return to Sodom and Gomorrah*. New York: Bible Studies & Archeologists, Random House.

Porter, C. (1934). *I Get a Kick Out of You*. Song written in 1934, recorded by Frank Sinatra in 1954 and 1962.

Prothero, S. (2010). *God Is Not One*. New York: Harper Collins
This is a good book to learn about many religions and philosophies.

Reitzer, D. (January 1, 2017). Gravitational theory proof. Canton, OH: The Canton Repository. A quote from the *Lincoln Star Journ*al.

Sagan, C. (1980). *Cosmos*. New York: Random House. Note: It was later produced as a TV series; as a personal voyage. It was a series of 13 episodes hosted by Carl Sagan on NPR.

Sagan, C. (1995). *A Demon-Haunted World: Science as a Candle in the Dark*. New York: Random House, Inc.

Sellers, P. (1979). *Being There*. Movie, Lorimar Productions. In the last scene, Chancey (Peter Sellers), walks on the water of a pond and sticks his umbrella down in the water.

Septimus, D. *Must a Jew Believe in God?* From a discussion paper. This paper was given to me by Neal Libster, by the way of Rabbi Aronson in 2018. URL: *My Jewish Learning*. No date provided on url. EKS Publishing, Oakland, CA.

Septimus, D. *Awe and Religion*. Source a publication from Temple Israel.

*Shadowlands.* (1993). Movie, released in U.S. through Spelling TV, CBS TV Studios, Los Angeles, CA.

*Tech Insider. (November 9, 2015).* Jennifer Welch. New York: Insider, Inc.

*The Lord's Prayer, Matthew (6:5-15, Luke 11:1-13). St. James Version.*

*Toward the Liberally Educated Executive.* U.S. Department of Education: Fund for Adult Education.

Trueblood, D.E. (1957). *Philosophy of Religion.* New York: Harper Brothers.

Truss, L. (2003). *Panda Eats, Shoots and Leaves.* London, Eng: *Profile Books, Ltd.*
The story is included on the book jacket about the pandas.

Twain, M. (1963). *Letters from Earth*, edited by Bernard DeVoto. New York: Crest Books, Fawcett World Library, by arrangement with Harper & Row.

Tyson, N. (2017). *Astrophysics for People in a Hurry.* New York: W.W. Norton & Co.

Tyson, N. (2014). *Cosmos: A Spacetime* on NPR for the 21st century.

*USA Today*. (November 30, 2010). TV show. Doug Stangling. McLean VA: Gannett & Co.
They have over 37 publishing locations.

Von Daniken, E. (1968). *Chariots of the Gods*. New York: Putnam & Sons Books.
Von Daniken wrote a number of books defending his hypothesis.

Wells, S. (2002). *The Journey of Man: A Genetics Odyssey*. Princeton, NJ: Princeton University Press.

Wells, S. (2003). *The Journey of Man*. TV movie. Washington, D.C. & Miami: www.pbs.org.

Worrell, F. (1958). *Religiosity and Humanitarianism Among Hi-Y Clubs in Akron, Ohio*.
Unpublished thesis. Kent State University.

CPSIA information can be obtained
at www.ICGtesting.com
Printed in the USA
LVHW070223130520
655495LV00025B/317/J